THE BETRAYAL OF THE SELF

Arno Gruen

—THE—
BETRAYAL OF THE SELF
The Fear of Autonomy in Men and Women

With a Preface by Gaetano Benedetti
and a Foreword by Ashley Montagu

Translated from the German by
Hildegarde and Hunter Hannum

GROVE PRESS
New York

Published by Grove Press, Inc.
920 Broadway
New York, N.Y. 10010

Library of Congress Cataloging-in-Publication Data

Gruen, Arno.
The betrayal of the self.

Translation of: Der Verrat am Selbst.
Bibliography: p.
Includes index.
1. Autonomy (Psychology) 2. Oppression (Psychology)
3. Control (Psychology) I. Title.
BF575.A88G7813   1988   155.2'32   86-45253
ISBN 0-8021-1017-7

Designed by Irving Perkins Associates, Inc.
Manufactured in the United States of America
First Edition 1988
10 9 8 7 6 5 4 3 2 1

CONTENTS

FOREWORD

TO be born human is to be born in danger, because everything we come to know and do *as human beings* we must learn from others. Furthermore, because we are the most impressionable, flexible, and malleable of all creatures, we are capable of being taught; learning not only more that is sound but also more that is unsound than any other living creature. The result is not intelligence, but confusion. Our socializers, parents, teachers of every kind, bent on perpetuating the errors which have been visited upon them by their socializers, and perceiving them as the eternal truths pertaining to the raising and disciplining of children, commit—with more or less the best of intentions—the most awful atrocities upon their victims. The awfulness of these atrocities consists of inflicting upon the child a deformation process called "upbringing," or "raising the child," which is no less than a crippling of the child's potentialities for the realization of its uniquenesses and its basic behavioral needs: the need for love, friendship, imagination, curiosity, song, dance, explorativeness, experimental-mindedness, open-mindedness, the need to learn, to work, to play, to think, to speak, and many others. These are all potentialities, which the child strives to realize through the encouragement of love, the love of the caregivers. This is no longer theory, but a fact which has now been verified countless numbers of times. I have set out the scientific facts in my book *Growing Young* (1983).

In an adult-made world the child is treated as an intruder, an alien, who has to conform to the external requirements of his socializers instead of the internal requirements of his own system of values, which are his basic behavioral needs or drives, and which cry out for the loving encouragement toward their fulfillment. But what the child usually receives is a rather dusty answer: the imposition of the selves of the socializers upon the *Anlage*, the potentialities, the basic behavioral needs, which constitute the foundations of the child's unique self. The result is that what we call the self is an artificial artifact, an inauthentic self, which the individual has forced upon him, and which he wears like an ill-fitting garment, awkwardly and uncomfortably. We have all more or less suffered this experience, and some of us have suffered more than others, sometimes to the point of behavioral or physical destruction. In the Western world, at least, we do not learn to become our true selves, to become ourselves, but to become a confusion of other people's selves, false, inauthentic selves. Thus deformed, we go through life attempting to play the roles that are expected of us. This can be very trying. As E. M. Forster put it in *A Room With A View,* "Life, wrote a friend of mine, is a public performance on the violin, in which you must learn the instrument as you go along." Very few of us succeed, and the resulting noise is harrowing. It is noise that the child learns, unwanted sound, words that are disordered, and disordering and dis-autonomizing. And thus it comes about that the child, living in a world he never made, in a sick society, powerless and helpless, ruled by rulers, comes to feel toward adults much as the inhabitants of an occupied country feel toward the occupiers. It is a feeling that the adult scarcely ever is able to throw off, and in most therapeutic situations that is the period with which one begins. And so we go on living by the will of the occupiers rather than by our own.

I know of no book that makes all this so beautifully clear as Gruen's. It is one of those fundamental books that is likely to prove a landmark in the history of the study of human nature and the human consequences of living in the kind of cubistically dilapidated environments of the Western world. The author's conclusions, set so illuminatingly before us, are based upon years of experience with patients and have been tested upon the anvil of teaching. Gruen writes about profoundly important and complex matters with that wonderful simplicity which only writers of great understanding and deep sympathy achieve. In so doing he opens up to the view an undiscovered territory of human experience, which, though approached by others, has never been so ably and illuminatingly explored, an exploration that will excite and help the reader to understand, perceive, and traverse this new world which Gruen has opened up.

I have been astonished and unendingly admiring of the profound insights of the author into the nature of what we ambiguously call human nature, and by the profound insights and skill with which he relates them to our everyday lives, and all this in language both memorable and quotable.

Gruen has a gift for the apt phrase and the striking aphorism, and in this as in the whole book he has been exceptionally well served by his translators. Altogether *The Betrayal of the Self* is one of those rare books which is as original as it is interesting, sound, and readable. I cannot recommend it too highly. It is a book I shall read and reread for the sheer pleasure of its rare combination of wisdom and insight into the causes and effects of our present state of confusion and the cure which so clearly suggests itself for the slough of despond into which we have fallen.

ASHLEY MONTAGU

PREFACE

THE roots of evil, of negativity, of psychopathology are manifold. The author of this book, a psychotherapist of broad experience, investigates them from a specific, highly significant point of view: the blocking of autonomy in the socialization process.

"The type of personal integration we attain," we read on the very first page of the author's introduction, "is a consequence of the possibilities we have of developing autonomy in our life situation. Thus, a distorted development of autonomy is the root cause of the pathological and, ultimately, evil element in human beings."

This use of the term "autonomy" originated, as we know, with Erik Erikson, in whose thinking it represents—quite correctly—only one dimension, albeit a very important one, of psychological growth. Underlying it is "basic trust."

What we need today, however, is an investigation of the distorted forms an individual's development can take when psychological growth is stunted. It is in this area that Arno Gruen makes such a valuable contribution, encompassing as he does the whole spectrum from the pathological in a strict psychiatric sense to psychosocial abnormality occurring within the bounds of the norm (what the author calls "the madness of mental health").

The present work is the fruit of its author's long career as psychotherapist, which I have had the opportunity to follow for a number of years as it has found step-by-step expression in a series of articles. His central insights are in agreement with essential aspects of the form of psychotherapy I myself practice with psychotics—and as a matter of fact it was Gruen's treatment of psychotic patients that led to many of his own findings.

In particular, we share the insight that what is described as psychopathology involves not only the loss of autonomy as a basic dimension of human existence but also an abnormal form of it which is fraught with suffering. For a profound need in our patients, not integrated in their childhood during the socialization process, can "go underground" (Gruen) and be expressed, for example, as a psychotic delusion, which may be seen as symbolic of the fact that there was no room in "reality" for the societal realization of their basic desires, drives, and, thus, for the full unfolding of their egos.

Sometimes, however, suffering does not ensue, and people adapt to the reality of power that stifles all possibility of creativity and autonomy. In situations like these we see a fundamental perversion of human existence: such persons flourish biopsychically at the expense of others, whose psychological needs—whose identity and ability to create—they totally smother.

When our patients' suffering does appear, it no longer strikes us simply as a negative sign, merely as a "betrayal of the self" (although it is that too) by the individual and his or her society; we also find in it a desperate attempt, on the part of those who have been betrayed and have cooperated in this betrayal, to assert their unfulfilled and not even consciously recognized desire for autonomy in the immature and distorted form of psychopathology—in this form even to shout it from the housetops, as it were. For such a desire has to be proclaimed in some manner, since our basic human impulses can never be completely extinguished.

Our approach means that we have learned, in all those cases where our patients' autonomy has been forced to express itself pathologically, to view symptoms and negative qualities as symbols of thwarted but unmistakably audible basic human desires. Indeed, it is impossible *not* to hear what our patients are expressing in the form, common to all psychopathology, of negation of the norm. Once we take note of their messages—not only as psychotherapists but also as fellow human beings—we give the symptom that "reception" (Siirala) which may bring about change. We restore to our patients a consciousness of their loss of autonomy and thus make possible their recognition of the existential tragedy involved. We hold up for our suffering partners a sympathetic mirror image in which they can find themselves. We begin to have hopes for them and with them. "It is sympathy and love that make possible the unfolding of the true self" (Gruen).

These and similar concerns of Arno Gruen's important book place it at the heart of the spiritual situation of modern men and women and also undoubtedly of contemporary writings on psychotherapy. Is it merely an accident that the question of autonomy is being discussed today in so many different fields—in the area of political emancipation as well as in that of the psychotherapeutic endeavor? Consider, to take just one example, that even hypnosis—that old form of psychotherapy which appeared to be diametrically opposed to all strivings for autonomy (therapeutic suggestions were forced upon passive patients in order to free them from their symptoms)—has undergone a revolution since Milton Erikson: it is now seen as a situation in which new, autonomous, creative learning is possible. According to this view, even the hypnotic trance has become a place where psychic potentialities and abilities can be developed.

Arno Gruen's book, like the works of Erich Fromm in this respect, far transcends the confines of psychiatry because it also treats the human condition in contemporary society and describes the psychopathology lurking behind "the mask of mental health." It denounces that betrayal of the self which is causing the downfall of individuals and whole groups. "It is," the author tells us, "our fate, if we never had the chance to rebel, to live with the absurdity of never having experienced a self of our own."

GAETANO BENEDETTI

INTRODUCTION

THIS work presents the reader with a theory of autonomy which maintains that being autonomous does not result from having *ideas* of one's own importance, nor from the necessity for independence, but from being able to experience freely one's own perceptions, feelings, and needs. This kind of experience determines the unity or the dissociation of personality development.

The type of personal integration we attain—or the effective lack thereof—depends on what possibilities our life situation offers us for the development of autonomy. It is a distorted development that is the root cause of the pathological and, ultimately, evil element in human beings.

The struggle for autonomy heightens our aliveness. Insofar as the socialization process blocks autonomy, however, this process engenders the evil it attempts to prevent. If parental love is so distorted that it demands submission and dependence for its self-confirmation, social adjustment turns into a test of obedience and the child's efforts to comply bring with them the loss of genuine feelings. The human being then becomes the true source of evil. Yet it is a paradox of our nature that the failure to attain autonomy may also represent a nonfailure. For autonomy can go underground and hide beneath subjection and submissiveness, beneath a surrender of self to the will of others. This is a hopeful sign.

In my first chapter I describe the nature of autonomy; in the second I attempt to show how our tendency toward abstraction masks and smothers the natural drive for autonomy; in the third my goal is to demonstrate that this tendency lies at the heart of the male's need to oppress women, but also of his own dehumanization. My fourth chapter shows how all this in turn reduces people's access to their own past, thereby making them more and more dependent on externally applied stimulation—they thus become stimulus-bound and robotlike. In my fifth chapter I investigate the way the frustration of autonomy leads to psychological "pathology" and simultaneously blinds us to the madness of the struggle for power. Finally, the sixth chapter portrays the way we shift morality to the plane of intellectual concepts while seeing evil as emanating directly from human nature. These distortions encourage the flight into the "image" and pseudo-feelings, and lead to the lack of an autonomous self, thereby producing human beings who destroy life.

This book is written in the hope of strengthening the resolve of those whose eyes are still open, in a world of conformity and adjustment, to the possibility of other human worlds. It is my desire here to help restore the sphere of feeling—in contrast to thinking and understanding, which are split off from feeling—to its rightful place in our scientifically oriented culture.

The present work is based on my thirty-five years of experience with psychotherapy. For this reason I would like to thank those people who were and still are a part of this experience and the learning that accompanied it: my patients and students both in Europe and in the United States; my teachers and friends, especially Gustav Bychowski, Thomas N. Jenkins, Theodore C. Schneirla and Henry Miller. The latter's authenticity and vitality were particularly important for my maturation as a human being, as were the acuity and originality of Schneirla's thinking. From my daughters Margaret and Constance, with their militant and loving spirit, I have also learned a great deal.

This book could not have been written without the creative, positive, and critical assistance of my partner in life, Ruth Schmidhauser. I therefore dedicate it to her.

I would like to express my sincerest thanks to Claus D. Eck, Claudia M. von Monbart, and Franz Wurm for their stylistic assistance with my manuscript. For the first edition I had the help of Ruth von Blarer. Her intuitive grasp of my intentions and her feeling for the needs of the reader made working with her a stimulating experience. I am deeply grateful to her for this. For stylistic checking of the German paperback edition I am very indebted to my editor Ulrike Buergel-Goodwin. The pages that follow are clearer as a result of her effort.

ARNO GRUEN

Ticino, 1985

THE BETRAYAL OF THE SELF

I

Autonomy and Adjustment: The Basic Contradiction in the Development of the Self

The Problem of Autonomy: Learning to Experience Emptiness

HUMAN development may follow one of two paths: that of *love* or that of *power*. The way of power, which is central in most cultures, leads to a self that mirrors the ideology of domination. This is a fragmented, split self that rejects suffering and helplessness as signs of weakness and emphasizes power and control as means of denying helplessness. The attainment of what passes for success in our world presupposes a self of this nature. Such a situation represents the antithesis of autonomy, which I now propose to discuss.

Autonomy is that state of integration in which one lives in full harmony with one's feelings and needs. Commonly we think of autonomy as something else, as something having to do with the assertion of one's own importance and independence. This applies particularly to the kind of self that, consciously or unconsciously, conforms to the ideology of domination. For this reason, what is commonly described as autonomy fits a concept of the self composed of abstractions. Although capable of rebellion, such a self is merely a reflection of those types of constricting, distorting, selfish qualities that parents, school, and society have imprinted within us. Autonomy is then equated with the "freedom" of constantly having to prove to ourselves and others how strong and superior we are. Whether such "proof" complies with or opposes existing norms makes no difference. What is important is that we must always be proving ourselves; this leads to a warlike stance, far removed from one in which we are able to affirm life. In contrast, having access to life-affirming emotions, to feelings of joy, sorrow, pain—in short, to a sense of being truly alive—is essential for the development of autonomy as I understand it.

The history of our culture is to a large extent one of avoidance, rejection, and suppression of these feelings and the needs they awaken. The oppression of women can be seen as a parallel expression of this phenomenon in our history: it is the access women have to sorrow and pain and their ensuing genuine vitality that, in society's eyes, must be combatted in them and in men of kindred spirit. The result: men, far more than oppressed women, are impaired in their humanity.

Autonomy entails having a self with access to its own feelings and needs. Since, in the case of the faulty development of autonomy, feelings and needs may express the ideology of domination rather than an inner integration, we must recognize that needs and feelings by themselves should not be equated with autonomy. It is important to analyze in detail the way autonomy develops.

It can be said that we learn to recognize ourselves in the mirror of our mother's eyes. The German dramatist Friedrich Hebbel put it poetically:

> Thus wondrously within your eyes
> I saw myself unfold.

This means that the mother's consciousness and her self-image are the determining factors in the development of our own self.

To the extent that she has failed to develop an adequate autonomy of her own, her self-esteem will be based on feelings and needs far removed from a truly autonomous position. As a consequence, the way she regards her own child—and thus how the child later sees itself in her eyes—will necessarily reflect these limitations. In this process we also find the origins of those forms of hatred and rage that often pass for love or self-sacrifice in our world.

We find a striking example of this is Jean Liedloff's *The Continuum Concept* (1985)[1]: the author is describing the situation of an infant who has recently been brought home from the maternity ward. His mother "loves him with a tenderness she has never known before. At first, it is hard for her to put him down after his feeding, especially because he cries so desperately when she does. But she is convinced that she must, for her mother has told her (and *she* must know) that if she gives in to him now he will be spoiled and cause trouble later. . . . She hesitates, her heart pulled toward him, but resists and goes on her way. He has just been changed and fed. She is sure he does not *really* need anything, therefore, and she lets him weep until he is exhausted" (pp. 62–63).

We see here a mother who does not recognize her child's longing for contact and touching and therefore cannot react appropriately. This can happen only because in *her* development her own longing was smothered, with the result that such a mother has no access to her own autonomy and consequently none to her child's. Something unspoken is taking place under the surface here: the mother allows her baby to suffer without having to be aware of what she is doing or having to admit to any motive behind her behavior. What Liedloff shows us is the appalling way we use our relationship to reality as a weapon to torment our children. We are dealing here with a denial of hostility, a denial that surrounds us from birth and is therefore unrecognized either by its victim or by the person who demands submission. There is *really* nothing wrong with the child!

In this way we need not face the fact that we are not only involved in repeating our own life history, our own experiences of being oppressed and violated, but that we are also smothering our own needs by this behavior. A baby's wails awaken in us our own despair of long ago and with it tormenting feelings of rage and powerlessness. We cannot admit to these feelings, however, for they contradict the view of "reality" we have been taught and the entire structure of our self based on it. To perceive a child's wails as signals of despair would threaten us with the breakdown of our psychic equilibrium. This is why we remain faithful to the perspective of our parents, who soothe and comfort us in those very areas in which we betray our self. And so we torment our children for reawakening the memory of our own deprivation. We silence them in a multitude of ways, for we are firmly anchored in "reality" and must defend it. Moreover, our domination of the helpless child provides one method of inflating our sense of self, our self-esteem. Power, domination, and control over others, including our children, give significance to our self.[2]

If we observe the situation of infants from this point of view and ask ourselves what their first learning experience consists of, we come to an unavoidable conclusion: they learn that there is *nothing* to be learned. They learn *not* to make their own reactions the point of departure for their development. This experience of learning that *there is nothing to be learned* is the decisive factor in the failure to develop autonomy; it is the first step in a distorted development, during which all we learn is to experience our own needs as something dangerous, even hostile. Autonomy and everything that could lead to it will then soon arouse feelings of fear.

This phenomenon is hidden from us, since the dominant patterns of thought (and theories of learning as well) regard learning as a process essentially determined from the outside. It occurs, according to the common view, when the organism is exposed under various conditions to this or that external stimulus. Current attitudes are far from recognizing that the motivation for learning might be a different one, one proceeding from inner processes characterized by a positive response to the surrounding world on the part of the organism. If we consider the relationship of a living being to its environment as a *meshing* (a joining of parts that fit together) and not as a mechanical process forced upon it, then learning will not be merely reaction to a stimulus but a search on the part of the reaction (and the needs underlying it) for stimuli suited to trigger the reaction. Seen in these terms, learning is not only an externally imposed procedure but a network of interwoven strands.

The opposite of this interpretation derives from a cybernetically inspired theory—as advanced, for example, by B. F. Skinner in his book *Beyond Freedom and Dignity* (1971)—that defines the human being in simplistic terms of mechanical *input* and *output*. Unfortunately, this is the type of thinking we are confronted with in many areas of the social sciences.[3] For this reason, we do not even become aware of the one-sided nature of the conventional approach to learning unless we are prepared to recognize autonomy as a viable possibility.

The True Path to Autonomy

Research done by DeCasper and Fifer (1980) shows not only that infants in the first three days of life already possess the ability to distinguish their mother's voice from other voices but that they also attempt to produce the mother's voice by means of mouth movements while sucking. This demonstrates that the capacity for autonomous behavior plays an integrative role from the very beginning of life. What happens, however, when the mother does not react appropriately, when she does not respond lovingly to the child's demands? This can mean only that the individual will be unable from the very outset to develop an integrated personality. The infant will be totally deprived of the possibility of learning anything about its own nature.

A mother is not necessarily conscious of her lack of an appropriate response. Vuorenkoski and colleagues (1969) observed the effects of infants' crying on the milk flow of first-time mothers. A recording of an infant crying was played for seven minutes: of the forty mothers studied, sixteen reacted within four minutes after the crying began; sixteen within seven minutes; four not until one minute after crying ended; and four not at all. If a mother is effectively cut off from her earliest feelings, she will not be able to empathize with her baby. It will be impossible for her to be sufficiently aware of its needs and its attempts to communicate with her. It is bad enough that her inadequate response interferes with the infant's nourishment; we can imagine how much worse the case will be if the child's needs, expressions of its drive for autonomy, provoke the mother to suppress her own and her child's.

Only if we are able to recognize that such interactions occur in countless variations in the first weeks of life and are instrumental in helping or hindering the emergence of an individual's essential being will we also grasp that our own responses determine the nature of the self very early in life. If the self is not permitted to develop independently, it will be formed by the will of the mother. Parents who are not able to respond to the actual needs of their children will cause their future integration to be dependent on the external world. The choice that is made for children at an early age is whether the development of the self (the organization of one's personality) will be formed by inner or by outer forces—in other words, whether they will live an autonomous existence or one dependent on external stimulation.

We see here the way autonomy can be destroyed, and that is not all that happens. The knowledge that nothing comes from within grows into a positive reinforcement of a negative situation; we learn not to recognize our own needs and motives. We cannot recognize our innermost self because we are not conscious of our own center. To this is added fear of the vital force of our own needs, which are experienced as dangerous enemies.

This state comes about because emptiness represents a psychological abyss. The accompanying feelings of helplessness, as well as the dismay and rage stemming from them, are vehemently rejected by the surrounding world. The rage, in actuality a direct expression of the self's vitality, changes into apathy and depression; when its direct expression is denied, children give up their enthusiasm for life and wither away inside. They then frequently learn to direct this rage against their drive for autonomy. By means of such displacement they create the preconditions for being rewarded by society. Once they submit in this manner to the will of others—their parents, for example—they will have no other choice but to direct their rage against everything that might even faintly awaken the drive for autonomy.

The more this course of events characterizes children's development, the more they will strike out against everything inside and outside themselves that might activate their vitality. Accordingly, they will first of all turn against other children and later, in adulthood, against youth in general. Their own perceptions, their own reality will be forced underground, and the boundaries of their self will be surrendered. Paradoxically, then, it will be precisely the first signs of feelings and needs of their own—in other words, the most deeply personal part of an individual—that will make their lives seemingly impossible. Their humanity, the ability to sense their own pain and that of others, represents a threat under these circumstances. People who have grown up in this way can neither recognize nor respect what Erik Erikson (1964) once described as the capacity to stand pain, to understand and alleviate suffering and recognize it as a fundamental aspect of common human experience.

Empathy as a Catalyst of Autonomy

How does the human capacity for empathy come about? Our most basic and profound method of communicating is an empathic one. The infant's connection to its environment is characterized by being held, carried, and touched. The kinesthetic nerve paths are the bearers of our direct perception of others; they are mutually modified by our visual, acoustic, tactile, and olfactory senses.[4] In his book *Young Man Luther* (1958), Erikson gives a poetic description of how a mother teaches her nursing child "to touch the world with his searching mouth and his probing senses" (p. 208). By his empathic awareness of his mother's attentions, the child becomes capable of sensing, and thereby giving form to, his own feelings by using his mother as a mirror. The complementary relationship between infant and mother is constantly modified by the changing nature of mutual recognition between the two.

In this connection, Condon and Sander (1974) observed that infants not only follow voices but also move to their rhythm, and this within the first sixteen hours of life. This "dance" is stimulating for the mother who responds to it. It shows her that her baby is reacting, is being attentive to her in turn! And thus each alters and acknowledges the other in an ongoing mutual development. (Rosenblatt [1978] presented a brilliant analysis of this synchronization in the case of subprimate mammals. The focus of his theoretical and experimental study is the changing states of need of offspring and mother, which are interpreted ontogenetically.)

The learning experiences gained here are closely connected to the quality of the stimuli characterizing the structure of the mother-infant relationship. To test out the world empathically, the infant must first of all enjoy the possibility of a sustained approach to its environment. This can occur only if the environmental stimuli experienced are of a low level of intensity. In a long series of publications culminating in an essay entitled "An Evolutional and Developmental Theory of Biphasic Processes Underlying Approach and Withdrawal" (1959), Schneirla emphasizes that already at birth there exists a primitive biphasic organic basis for later sensory stimulation. Low stimulus intensities (in a relative sense) tend to evoke approach reactions; high intensities evoke withdrawal reactions with reference to the stimulus source. The differential in the arousal thresholds of antagonistic sets of muscles performing these different reactions becomes the determinant of the developing behavioral patterns.

The result is encouragement of empathic processes, provided that closeness exists between infant and mother. Only if the mother is responsive to her child will the flow of low-intensity stimuli be assured. It is this which not only allows the child to thrive[5] but also provides the basis for its empathic sensory development.

This maternal responsiveness prevents the child from being overwhelmed by excessive stimulation. Fuller (1967) shows in his article on experiential deprivation that an organism can learn nothing in a given stimulus complex if it cannot be attentive to pertinent components of this complex by disregarding others.[6] Here we have the essence of a type of learning leading to autonomy. For such learning to take place, differentiation is necessary. This will not come about if the infant's inner readiness to respond cannot find an appropriate eliciting stimulus.[7]

A mother who intuitively protects her child from being flooded by stimuli is planting the seeds from which self-motivated learning can grow. If the mother is not in a position to do this, either the child's consciousness will be dominated by the experience of helplessness, which will lead to psychological crippling, or the feeling of utter defenselessness will be repressed and split off from the growing self. If the latter occurs, children will block out everything reminiscent of the situation in which they experienced these feelings, thus reducing their capacity for empathy and, consequently, their humanness. In this manner, entire parts of their developing self will be split off from consciousness. For the split to be sustained, helplessness must become an object of rejection and hatred. Helplessness is what seems threatening and *not* the situation which brought it about. As a result, people will continue to seek revenge on everything that might recall their own helplessness. That is why they scorn it in others. Scorn and contempt conceal their fear and at the same time encourage a general attitude of contempt for helplessness and the need for a compensatory ideology of power and domination. In this way, victims join the ranks of their oppressors in order to find new victims—an endless process by which human beings become dehumanized.

Thus, everything that could nurture one's own autonomy is despised. A relentless drive for success and achievement replaces the impetus toward autonomy. But such people reject the urge for autonomy not only because it might remind them of their own acquiescence but also because genuine autonomy unmasks the power structure they have adapted to in order to escape their helplessness. Since we are all victims of these circumstances to a certain extent, the result is an overall tendency toward dehumanization, even if this is not our intent at all. Our empathy is undermined every day, even—as in Liedloff's example—under the guise of solicitude. In such cases we do not notice that we ourselves are involved in distorting and falsifying our empathic perceptions of what is actually taking place in other people.

A typical example of this can be seen in the life of the founder of psychoanalysis: it is well known that Freud reacted with anger and indignation when he learned that those around him were hesitant to tell him the truth about his cancer. As a result, we find repeated references in psychoanalytic literature to weaknesses in Freud's character. Heinz Kohut, for one, in his book *The Restoration of the Self* (1977) maintains that Freud was incapable of realizing that kindness and concern might have been behind the hesitance to tell him the whole truth. Kohut comes to the conclusion that Freud's "nuclear self was threatened" (p. 65)—in other words, "injured narcissism"!

It is striking, in this interpretation, the way the application of psychoanalysis in the hands of many of its practitioners mirrors the ideology of domination. "Of course" there are no grounds for indignation if solicitude itself becomes an instrument of power. *Those who rebel against this situation will shatter the structure in which kindliness and caring are utilized to keep others in a state of dependency.* By giving our approbation to the traits of concern and caring, we merely disguise the true state of affairs. Freud cannot be granted his right to self-esteem and autonomy because if he were, it would be an admission that what we commonly take for therapy and humaneness is actually role-playing. Patients are expected to be grateful and to behave in a dependent manner. If they do so, they win the approval of their therapist, and their dependency— even if it takes an aggressive and uncooperative form—underscores the superiority of the therapist, who is the source of "kindness."

Freud's indignation meets with disapproval because it calls into question an attitude that is strongly cultivated both in the world of therapy and in general human relationships. The point of view exemplified by the mother in Liedloff's example and by Kohut's interpretation reflects that institutionalized pattern of behavior typified by dominating and being dominated. The hatred this pattern gives rise to destroys human autonomy.

We are all caught up to some extent in these circumstances. All of us have experienced helplessness, and the more negatively it has affected us—to the point of making a new and positive integration with our world impossible—the more we have come to fear it for also forcing us into a state of submission. But some of us refuse to relinquish our possibilities for becoming autonomous. I shall now discuss some of the forms that refusal takes.

Ways of Camouflaging Autonomy

It is paradoxical that the inner struggle to preserve autonomy can express itself in desperate adaptation, submission, and self-destructive behavior. Consequently, the form autonomy takes may make it impossible for the observer to recognize its existence or its nature as a fundamental life-force. This will be the case wherever it is met with indifference or is explicitly rejected. We should not be surprised that in societies demanding obedience, conformity, and dependency as the price of love, autonomy—as the most essential integrative factor in human development—is either denied or camouflaged.

A patient once said to me, "You cannot touch me if I am as you wish" (Gruen 1974, 1976). With unusual perspicacity he was able to intuit the thoughts and wishes of other people. By accommodating himself to their wishes, he protected himself from the perils of openness or commitment. He simply performed what others expected of him; he himself was not involved in his actions. Because he never displayed a will of his own, he thought of himself as inviolable and felt "free." But of course he was only potentially free, for he never translated his ideas into actions. Thus, his autonomy existed only in his own imagination.

Here we have an example of autonomy going underground, so to speak, in order to remain invulnerable, in this case by means of a total willingness to be submissive. Similarly, another patient of mine struggled against being manipulated by developing feelings of guilt in a specific way. In so doing, he became exactly the way he was expected to be. One day he said to me: "When I feel guilty, it's reassuring, it's safe, because you are not free to be you. Things are then dictated to you. Someone else dictates how you have to behave and you are safely in hiding. You can keep your superiority and contempt to yourself."

His guilt feelings, which functioned as a last possible form of contact with an otherwise inaccessible mother, also served, however, to keep his potential self out of her reach. By becoming an object of her will through feeling guilty, he was able to shield his own will from her manipulation. It was a vain effort on his part— and highly detrimental to the further course of his development—to preserve an autonomous stance by means of a fantasized invulnerability. If we misread here the covert nature of his attempt to gain autonomy by interpreting it simply as an expression of primary dependency, we will not be able to understand such a person's struggles, nor will we be able to acknowledge the validity of the drives for autonomy, which—even though repressed—are still at work.

In the field of ethology as well, the denial of these drives has led to distorted and false results. In 1967 the American zoologist J. L. Kavanau showed in a critical study of research methodology that experimental conditions are more likely to be set up to confirm the scientists' preconceived ideas than to reveal information about the laboratory animals' actual reactions (and about their relevant background). Animals, for example, which (for the sake of classification) are forced into a restricting situation for the purposes of an experiment, display reactions that are interpreted by the observer as incorrect. From the perspective of the behavior of the animals in question, however, these "incorrect" reactions represent enriching variations within their experimentally controlled environment. What for the animal is an adaptive reaction to restricting circumstances—a reaction that extends its sphere of activity in learning to deal with a maze by avoidance and modification, for instance—is seen by the observer as incorrect behavior, which is supposed to be a source of information about the animal's learning processes or its biological needs. Scientists are required to look at an animal's behavior from the standpoint of their theoretical paradigms—the animal's own life and vitality don't interest them. The animal's "mistakes" in this case are actually artifacts of experimental conditions specific to the scientist rather than to the animal. Kavanau is illustrating here what most ethologists are compelled to deny as a result of their prejudices: the indisputable fact that in life there are forces which resist the imposition of coercive circumstances.

Many facets of human development reflecting our efforts to become autonomous remain hidden, for autonomy finds various ways of concealing itself even within conformity. Our culture, with its major emphasis on adaptation, causes autonomy to camouflage its motivation. This in turn disguises the fact that human development is distinguished by the quest for autonomy.

Even Freud, whose revolutionary and bold thinking expanded our view of human nature and gave it a new direction, adopted an ambivalent attitude in these matters. For him, human development was a process that curbs our drives by means of repression, control, or sublimation. Developmental disorders were therefore seen as failures in one's capacity to adapt. He regarded drives as unalterable and basically evil instincts, which could be restrained only by socialization (Gruen and Hertzman 1972). Not only was adaptation to existent reality the goal of development but pathological symptoms were interpreted as the failure to adapt to this "reality," the validity of which was not questioned: those who were ill had to bear the onus for being ill. Given such an intellectual framework, it was impossible to recognize that pathological symptoms in the face of the pseudorealities of a given society may often be the only possible method of keeping autonomy alive.

We find a different view of the situation if we turn to the experiences of artists who see their development in terms of an inner struggle for authenticity. Anton Chekhov, for example, wrote to a young author:

> Write a story, do, about a young man, the son of a serf, a former grocery boy, a choirsinger, a high school pupil and university student, brought up to respect rank, to kiss the hands of priests, to truckle to the ideas of others—a young man who expressed thanks for every piece of bread, who was whipped many times, who went without galoshes to do his tutoring, who used his fists, tortured animals, was fond of dining with rich relatives, was a hypocrite in his dealing with God and men, needlessly, solely out of a realization of his own insignificance—write how this young man squeezes the slave out of himself, drop by drop, and how, on awaking one fine morning, he feels that the blood coursing through his veins is no longer that of a slave but that of a real human being. (Chekhov 1973, p. xiii)

Chekhov understood that hostility, malice, and sadism result from helplessness and self-contempt, that they are all produced by adapting to a hypercritical social reality and are not attributable to innate aggressiveness.

A schizoid patient explained to me after a period of psychotherapy that she now could see that all her life she had tried to be a nonentity, to be completely empty, except for some peanut shells she kept in her pocket so that if someone should hold her up (i.e., make a demand on her to perform and adjust), she could turn her pockets inside out and say, "You see, I have nothing worthwhile taking." Here we find the expression of an extreme defense against manipulation, even though it takes on a highly desperate and self-crippling form. The patient refused to exhibit conventional behavior, which might have implied that she had experienced an untroubled upbringing and that her mother had treated her with affection. She refused to confirm by her behavior the image of her mother as "loving and good." By acting as if all her decisions revolved only around other people's wishes—which she then, however, constantly refused to comply with—she unfortunately did in fact remain completely empty all her life. The consequences of her behavior were total psychic asthenia and pseudodebility.

As long as we measure a person's psychological health by the degree to which he or she accepts social conventions, we will fail to see that under certain circumstances these conventions demand a submissive acceptance of errors and lies. The meaning of schizophrenics' experience, on the surface so difficult for us to relate to, will become clear to us only if we can see that they are reacting with painful sensitivity to a specific type of hypocrisy: under the mask of convention may lurk a societal demand that certain forms of violence—such as the attempt to inhibit us in all expression of our inner nature—be interpreted as benevolence, solicitude, or even love.

In his book *The Ways of the Will* (1966), the psychoanalyst Leslie Farber (a collaborator of Frieda Fromm-Reichmann's) describes an encounter between a hospitalized schizophrenic and a therapist which illustrates the patient's misdirected attempts to become autonomous. It also demonstrates the way such patients continually attempt to inform us about the distorted nature of social reality.

The therapist in question had a fountain pen, given to him by his father, that he was very attached to. In the course of a therapeutic session the pen awakened the interest of his otherwise not very communicative patient. When the therapist noticed this, he placed the pen in the patient's hand and suggested that he try it out. Encouraged by the patient's response, the therapist said he could keep the pen till the next day. In the following sessions, no mention was made of the pen. After a few weeks, the therapist asked about it and said he would like to have it back. The patient didn't answer. After about six weeks had gone by, the therapist explained that the pen meant a lot to him, was a present from his father, and that he wanted to have it back. He urged the patient to discuss the matter with him. The patient mumbled that the pen was lost and didn't say another word for the rest of the hour, whereas the therapist became more and more agitated and ended by shouting at the patient. The session concluded on this unpleasant note, and the patient returned to his room. Shortly thereafter, the therapist and two attendants stormed into the patient's room. While the attendants pinned him to the floor, the therapist searched for the pen. Of course he found it, and as he left the room, the patient shouted up at him from the floor, "My God, what a madhouse! All this fuss about one little fountain pen!" (p. 190).

Farber is trying to make clear in his report that although the therapist was a polite, civilized man, he still failed to realize the actual motives for his violent action, explaining his behavior in terms of the well-known psychoanalytic mechanism of transference. (In this interpretation, the countertransference consisted of the therapist becoming furious because he was treating the patient in a maternal manner out of a desire to cure him; when the patient did not respond positively to that treatment, he lost his temper.) Farber interprets the incident differently, for he sees the encounter as the collision of two wills. In my judgment, neither explanation does justice to the content of this encounter.

There is no doubt that the patient's behavior was provocative. But wasn't the therapist expecting his patient to join him in playing roles according to an established script with fixed but unexpressed rules? Wasn't it the patient's part, by acting "nice," to validate the therapist's self-image as a nice person—a kind, gentle, and loving man? Wasn't the therapist misusing the patient— the way we misuse one another day in and day out—in order to see his own virtue validated? It seems that he not only wanted to be a good mother; his generosity was also part of a game involving mutual validation, in the course of which one partner feels himself powerful and important while the other proves how obedient he can be.

Had the patient played along, wouldn't he too have proved by his "correct" behavior what a good patient he had become, one on the way to recovery? Of course he sensed all this and refused to cooperate. Schizophrenics[8] are often so uncooperative because, in defending themselves by their "helplessness," they unmask the hypocrisy of the playacting around them. This irritates us, for we are prisoners of our own script. Who has the right to be openly angry if others, in accordance with their role, respond to such "helplessness" only with kindness? The patient's behavior forces us to suffocate in our own playacting. In response, we take revenge by insisting on "helping." And if this has no effect, those who offer the help undergo a serious psychic crisis, which is often manifested in psychosomatic symptoms, such as migraine.

It is true that this patient turned a deaf ear to the therapist's human side, to his intention to be friendly and supportive. Yet such patients—with their unerring ability to unmask a constricting love as hypocrisy—give us a glimpse of the truth we deny every day. We all play a variety of roles, which serve the purpose of supporting systems designed to keep our image intact—systems based, in their turn, on power. By contributing to the strengthening of these systems we unwittingly demonstrate how often the ideology of power goes unchallenged. (Power may elicit resistance; the ideology behind it does not.) There is a self-perpetuating cycle at work here, which causes us to become more and more estranged from ourselves and keeps us from knowing what we are doing to ourselves and others. In our world it is those who are considered the most successful who adapt best to this pseudoreality. And those who adapt best are also the ones who are most cut off from their feelings. Paradoxically, success conceals the insanity of those who live cut off from their emotional world.

The result is a *reality* that Marcel Proust described as follows: "How can we have the courage to wish to live, how can we make a movement to preserve ourselves from death, in a world where love is provoked by a lie and consists solely in the need of having our sufferings appeased by whatever being has made us suffer?" The patient's recalcitrance was meant as a test and was simultaneously a refusal to take part in the mutual deception. A *helpless* schizophrenic can get away with this! Unfortunately, however, it will lead to a total loss of personal and social contact, to psychic suicide, since social convention brands *nonparticipation* as a type of treason.

The patient's refusal throws light on precisely what is ordinarily kept from our consciousness: those who dominate and those dominated, oppressors and oppressed are caught up in a power exchange in which solicitude leads to the restriction of freedom; to top it off, the whole transaction is then called love. The price of adapting to this course of events is a fear of one's own freedom and vitality, and this in spite of whatever display of rebellion may be made. We can be critical of and oppose society's norms without being conscious of this fear. Without noticing it, we have already surrendered our freedom, even to the point of unknowingly identifying with the power oppressing us. Fear of our own autonomy and of the vitality it produces becomes the unconscious focal point of our life. This fragmentation of our potential autonomy is so extensive in scope that we are not even aware of it.

Our Fear of Autonomy and of Freedom to Have a Self of Our Own

One example of the extensive fragmentation of autonomy and the accompanying unconsciousness of it may be observed in the way we run, walk, and stand—in other words, in our everyday body movements. (It is interesting in this connection that the movements of many schizophrenics strike us as a parody of the manner in which we move. They reflect a rejection of society's rules for our bodily behavior.)

In the lecture delivered upon receiving the Nobel Prize in 1973, Nikolaas Tinbergen (1974) analyzed the posture and movement of our bodies. He described how most of us go around with rigid neck muscles, hunched shoulders, and tensed buttocks muscles. We sit with a rounded back that we hold either too far to the front or the back. We have *definite ideas* about sitting, standing, and walking, and we try to follow them. Our conscious ideas about posture and movement mirror a static concept of balance more than its actual dynamic quality. If we have a *harmonious body feeling*, then the transition from one position to another—whether sitting, standing, or walking—is a flowing one. But as soon as we attempt to make our movements consciously, most of us will notice that we must prepare ourselves inwardly in order to change from one position to another.

Tinbergen was deeply impressed when he tried out a method of physical rehabilitation (the Alexander Method[9]) by how quickly his body control improved. Apparently, with the help of the right approach, we are able to rid ourselves of the constraints of our past.

Moshe Feldenkrais (1949, 1972, 1977), who studied human body movement for forty years, made similar observations about the learning capacity of the cerebral cortex (this is the organ through which we control bodily behavior). We evidently have the ability to *relearn rapidly* and can thus replace unsatisfactory movements with better integrated ones if new experiences come our way.

"Misuse, with all its psychosomatic, or rather somatopsychic, consequences," says Tinbergen, "must therefore be considered a result of . . . culturally determined stress" (p. 25). According to von Holst and Mittelstaedt (1950), it is apparently the brain's function to supply a "correct" idea of bodily performance. It seems likely that the results of our movements are sent back in the form of images to the brain, where they are then compared with expectations stored in the cerebral cortex. Tinbergen and Feldenkrais emphasize that the sources of these expectations are not genetic but phenotypic—that is, they are determined by early learning and socialization.

I call attention to these matters because in my judgment what is involved here is not only an incorrectly learned pattern of movement; more importantly, our way of walking and standing, conditioned by negative cultural influences, is only one part of a much larger phenomenon: *the substitution of another's will for our own* causes us to lose the ability to function autonomously. The consequences of such a universal substitution may be illustrated by a personal experience I had at a workshop for health professionals. It showed me not only that the occurrence is entirely repressed from consciousness but also how reluctant we are even to acknowledge this fact when it is brought to our attention.

The workshop, held in 1979 in the Children's Center of the Munich University Hospital, was on functional therapy and was led by Feldenkrais (Gruen 1980a). Early in his work on body movement, he came to the conclusion that the *pressure of socialization* has an inhibitory and limiting effect on learning ability. Rehabilitative work with patients suffering from cerebral palsy, multiple sclerosis, and other diseases indicated that specific thought patterns and faulty experiences with our body often cause loss of function. Forced upon us by the socialization process, these thought patterns steer our body toward adaptation, for that is what promises us social and therefore emotional security. Such thinking inevitably leads to the *splitting off of our body sensations*. And this kind of separation, which brings a *splitting of feelings* in its wake, makes it extremely difficult for a self to emerge on the basis of our *own experiences*. It was the goal of the workshop to introduce the participants to a form of integration built on new body experiences.

In two days, Feldenkrais brought a group of approximately one hundred specialists (doctors, psychologists, physical therapists) to the point of gaining control over their motility to such an extent that, sitting on the floor and pivoting in only one direction, they were able to encompass a visual angle of 360°. Our movements had been stemming from abstract concepts we have about the kind of actions possible for us; Feldenkrais enabled us to be so in harmony with our body that we could modify these movements once he reunited us with the bodily self from which we had become alienated.

I report both this episode and Tinbergen's ideas because immediately after our experience of liberation, general dissatisfaction broke out in the workshop group. Participants became critical of Feldenkrais, directing anger and aggression toward him. It was as though the sudden freedom itself had produced disquiet and anxiety.

The disturbing thing about our adaptation is not only that to some extent we all live involuntarily in accordance with the will of other people; what is really dangerous is that the moment we live *outside* the bounds of our body, so to speak, we begin to *fear the freedom* suddenly revealed by the breakthrough of our original sense of self. While it is true that we all long for freedom, in many ways we are simultaneously dependent on power, desiring recognition and praise from those who hold it. This condemns us to an eternal search for approbation from those very people who deny our real needs.

As already mentioned, we learn in earliest childhood to yield to the demands of those whose "love" we are dependent on. Without reflection, we learn *to equate freedom with disobedience*. Therefore, we respond to freedom, as Feldenkrais's workshop demonstrated, with anxiety and fear. The deeper significance of Proust's observation that we need to have our suffering appeased by those who have made us suffer must have its source here. If parents regard the vitality and zest for life of their young children as disturbing or even threatening, the children will soon be filled with uneasiness and anxiety.

Erich Fromm (1941) wrote about the escape from freedom on the political level, pointing out that freedom involves responsibility, which is something people would like to evade. It seems to me, however, that what undermines our chance for freedom is the fear going back to those early childhood years, characterized by uneasiness and anxiety, during which our own vitality and zest for life became our enemies. In other words, the self becomes the enemy. We want to escape responsibility because we are deeply afraid of having a self of our own. It is not an abstract responsibility we find threatening but rather the responsibility to realize ourselves. Our own vitality as well as that of others frightens us; if it still manages to surface, we respond with rage and turn against our own freedom. It is vitality itself that we are opposing.

The lesson of our childhood is that power, initially experienced at the hands of our parents, promises an escape from the helplessness we despise. It becomes the exemplary means of rescuing ourselves from feelings of inadequacy. Freedom then takes on an entirely different, unexpressed significance: it means deliverance from, not harmony with, our own needs. In this way the wish for freedom is perverted into a struggle for power, a struggle to gain mastery over things outside our rejected self. Possession of things and living beings—so the voices of our culture promise us—will bring security. In fact, however, the numerous artificial needs that then arise serve only to separate us even more from our true self.

Unfortunately, rebellion is no guarantee that this lesson will be revised. Identification with power as the way of deliverance binds us to the ideology of the oppressors.[10] We are impaired in exactly the same manner as our parents before us and as the society we are fighting against. We deny our genuine needs; we are afraid of our own self. And thus we remain allied with our enemy. In *The Time of the Assassins* (1956), a study of Rimbaud's greatness and failure, Henry Miller wrote that the freedom Rimbaud longed for entailed the unrestrained assertion of his ego. It is a self-assertion that provides a distorted reflection of what someone has been subjected to whose attempts at autonomy were denied by a ruthless exercise of power. He or she simply ignores the rights and individuality of others, but this time it is done under the guise of expressing one's freedom. "That," wrote Miller, "is not freedom. . . . It will never aid one to find one's link, one's communion, with all mankind" (p. 49). And the reason for this is that such people have been impaired in their capacity to feel. Rimbaud was the child of a cold and cruel mother who was unwilling to recognize his true nature. She was afraid of his vitality and warmth (when he was still a child); and he, although he wanted to "see all, feel all, exhaust everything, explore everything, say everything" (p. 29), longed in the end only for her approval. In spite of his rebellion, he capitulated to her coldness, to her fear of his vitality.

This is also the true trauma of our generation, which wants a better, more humane world but doesn't realize that its own wounded humanity stands in the way of its goal. In Miller's words: "All this has but one meaning for me—that one is still bound to the mother. All one's rebellion was but dust in the eye, the frantic attempt to conceal this bondage" (p. 49).[11] If we are split off from our needs, everything must be a struggle. We fear whatever might link us to our fellow human beings. Therefore, we yearn for something from those who cannot give us anything. We make demands on them without realizing that we are concealing our dependency in this way. And just like those we struggle against, we too make violence in its manifold forms the center of our existence.

In *Terror or Love?* (1977) Bommie Baumann describes dropping out of the German terrorist movement when he realized that terrorism itself is an attempt to escape from the need for love. Unlike his companions, he came from a working-class family, which may explain why he was not as split off from his feelings as his middle-class comrades. Nevertheless, Baumann and his companions unconsciously confused dependency with love. Thus, day after day they had to deny by their behavior a hidden dependence on their parents. Their impatient "I want it right now!" enabled them to deny this dependency. They used their ideology for the purpose of masking the impatience,[12] which was a form of revenge on their parents—parents who had given their sons and daughters everything but the love they needed. The children were spoiled in order to support the parents' false self-image. Without their knowing it, their rebellious impatience expressed a dependency based on the unacknowledged assumption that the world owed them the fulfillment of a vague, perstent, inexpressible longing. They were unable to recognize what it was that linked them with those they were so vehemently rebelling against—a secret mutual dependency—and thus they could remain true and obedient to the dictates of power. (Naturally, I am speaking here about rebellion in general and not about revolutionaries who have transcended both their bondage to authority and their simultaneous wish to dominate others.)

How Obedience Replaces Autonomy and Leads to Dehumanization

That complying with power and authority commonly leads to a denial of one's own human feelings was also demonstrated by Milgram's famous experiment conducted at Yale University in 1963. In this research project, the participants, middle-class residents of New Haven, were required to administer painful electric shocks to others taking part in the experiment; they were obeying scientific authorities who claimed that the shocks would benefit the recipients by helping them to learn a series of exercises.

With the exception of those few who simply refused to continue the experiment when its sadistic aspects became clear to them, all the others cooperated by obeying the command to administer shocks of increasing intensity. The director of the experiment, unquestioningly accepted as a scientific authority by most of the participants, said, "Press the lever, give the shock, it's for this person's good"—and the test subjects administered the shocks, even when the recipient cried out, began to jerk convulsively, and appeared to lose consciousness. They simply relinquished their natural empathy, although it can be gathered from the charts and reports of the experiment that empathy was present, for the majority of them developed psychosomatic symptoms during the procedure: they perspired, began to tremble, to stutter, bit their lips, had fits of nervous laughter. It is evident from the records that the test subjects in no way permitted their personal reactions to the suffering of their experimental victims to enter their consciousness.

To such an extent, then, can the adaptation process we find everywhere make us suppress our humanity. Yet, when a person's need to be human will still manifest itself—for instance, in the form of psychosomatic or so-called neurotic disorders—then such people can afford us insight into the inner workings of such processes.

A patient whose sensitivity to his personal and real needs had become a burden to him because it interfered with his adaptive capacities described his situation in these words: "My sensitivity gets me nowhere . . . it's just a burden to me . . . That man [he was speaking of an industrialist he admired whom he had met while on vacation] plays tennis and builds an empire for himself. What does it matter if he hasn't any feelings? I have the impression that he doesn't know what stomach pains are. Yes, I admire him because his goal in life is not to suffer from being sensitive but rather to be *in*sensitive . . . He and others like him don't have to worry about *reality* at all."

This illustration shows that many patients enter therapy not in order to preserve their human feelings, which they perceive as "a hindrance," but to be liberated from them. The way the Oedipus complex is treated in analysis often masks the therapist's collaboration with the patient in attempting to achieve this goal. Analysis that does not make patients confront their own helplessness and the ensuing betrayal of their autonomy conceals the true source of the Oedipal situation, which lies in the oppression of women and the consequent attempt of parents to gain importance and power by possessing their children (Gruen 1969; Sampson 1966). It is this possessive mentality, the use of children as pawns in a parental power struggle, that creates Oedipal guilt feelings. If psychoanalysis frees patients from these feelings without touching the deeper childhood trauma involved—namely, the impairment of the child's basic empathic (autonomous) nature—a personality will evolve whose drive for power now has nothing standing in its way.

The case of the patient discussed above illustrates clearly what it means to want a self that is predicated on power. He would like to have the power that would enable him to escape the reality of his own as well as others' feelings and needs. That is his idea of freedom (and, tacitly, society's as a whole): not to have to worry about this *reality*. He was merely articulating what is suggested to us every day either by the words or, implicitly, the deeds of those setting the social standards around us.

The obvious conclusion here is that in our society it is not those who suffer that are weak but those who fear suffering. People who have made the most successful societal adjustment actually turn out to be the weak ones. To conceal this fact, the "well-adjusted" have for millenia been propagating the myth that sensitivity means weakness. They are the ones who try to escape all pain and suffering by a split in their consciousness; they are the ones who perpetuate a distorted view of reality, that is, the ideology of power and domination.

In her book *Stilwell and the American Experience in China* (1971), the historian Barbara Tuchman reports a conversation Madame Chiang Kai-shek had with friends. The reality of power had been the determining factor in Madame Chiang's life. When her friends told her about the integrity, idealism, and self-sacrifice of the Chinese revolutionaries around Mao Tse-tung in Hunan Province in the forties, she made a statement that Tuchman calls the saddest she had ever heard: "If what you tell me about them is true, then I can only say they have never known *real* power"

(p. 185). This is the way a person who has had to betray her humanity for the sake of power expresses her suffering—if only for one conscious moment. Madame Chiang realized that power kills ideals.

The following item from the *New York Times* of February 7, 1968, shows us how desperate people can become if, after attempting to live all their life in obedience to the lie of power, they finally begin to resist:

> Phoenix, Arizona. February 6 (AP). Linda ... killed herself, policemen said today, rather than make her dog Beauty pay for her night with a married man.
>
> "I killed her. I killed her. It's just like I killed her myself," a detective quoted her grief-stricken father as saying.
>
> "I handed her the gun. I didn't think she would do anything like that." ... Linda failed to return home from a dance in Tempe Friday night. On Saturday she admitted she had spent the night with an Air Force Lieutenant.
>
> The [parents] decided on a punishment that would "wake Linda up." They ordered her to shoot the dog she had owned about two years.
>
> On Sunday, the [parents] and Linda took the dog into the desert near their home. They had the girl dig a shallow grave. Then [the mother] grasped the dog between her hands, and [the father] gave his daughter a .22-caliber pistol and told her to shoot the dog.
>
> Instead, the girl put the pistol to her right temple and shot herself.

Autonomy and Adaptation

The lack of development of the self in schizophrenics is a highly paradoxical expression of the drive for autonomy—operating underground, so to speak. If the drive is extinguished, however—

even if this occurs with the victim's consent—we will find in place of an underground autonomy the attempt to derive strength exclusively by identifying with the oppressing authority.[13] Adaptive behavior such as this creates the image of *normality*. There will be no struggle for self-realization. And since identification with power becomes the end goal of personal development instead of serving as a bridge to one's own individuality, the socialization process will inescapably be based on repression and sublimation.

If the emergence of a sufficient degree of autonomy is blocked, an underlying feeling of rage—both kindled and concealed by the dissociation of a growing feeling of helplessness—will furnish the parameters of the individual's development. Sigmund Freud's description of the socialization process applies here: these are the people who hate themselves because they haven't come to terms with their helplessness. They feel threatened by helplessness itself, not by those who caused or reinforced the feeling, and this is what produces their boundless rage. Therefore, they repress their helplessness, which has made them feel rejected and despised, at the same time internalizing their oppressors' contempt for them. In this way they commit betrayal of the self. Disguised hatred of themselves and everyone else—with the exception of those whose inhumanity makes them appear *strong*—becomes the guiding force in their life. For such persons, socialization is necessarily a process of repression.

An alternate path is pointed out to us by the social "failures"— those schizophrenics, nonachievers, rebellious children, and adolescents whom we treat as outcasts. Their despair is a response to the falseness of a love by which we seek to attain self-esteem, a self-esteem based not upon that part of us which is truly alive but upon the assertion of our power and importance. An illustration of an opposite process is found in Sophocles' drama *Philoctetes*, in which the young Neoptolemus lends his heartfelt support to the stinking, festering outcast Philoctetes and thus brings about the latter's return to human society. In Edmund Wilson's critical study *The Wound and the Bow* (1965), he points out that Ulysses believes he can appropriate the ailing Philoctetes' superhuman strength by acquiring his bow without having to acknowledge him as a human being. For Neoptolemus, whose task it is to carry out this act of manipulation, such conduct goes against nature. Because he, as Wilson writes, "is guileless enough and human enough to treat him, not as a monster, nor yet as a mere magical property which is wanted for accomplishing some end, but simply as another man, whose sufferings elicit his sympathy . . . he dissolves Philoctetes' stubbornness, and thus cures him and sets him free" (pp. 241–42).

Only if we don't treat those seeking help like objects we can possess, or use them as means to bolster our "self-esteem"; only if we approach them as human beings, not in order to have a sense of power over them but because their pain elicits our sympathy or their courage our admiration; only if we take the risk of recognizing the common humanity we share with them—only then will we be able to open up the path to their autonomy, especially in the case of the schizophrenic or the crying child.

Moreover, the clearer we are in our mind about these matters, the more successful we will be in resisting the pressure exerted on us always to doubt our own feelings and to be ashamed of our humane qualities. In this resides the real meaning for the growth of our consciousness: to endure in the struggle for our own reality in the face of the ubiquitous pressure to conform to a distorted and diminished "reality."

II

Abstraction: Its Role in Diminishing and Impairing Human Experience

ONE of the factors that gives rise to and perpetuates splitting of the self, as well as violence in our life, is abstraction. It is in part the overvaluation of intelligence which has made us glorify abstract thought—at the expense of passion, enthusiasm, and openness. Søren Kierkegaard noted in 1846 that when intelligence is overvalued to such a degree, it transforms reality into ideas which then come to take its place. This transformation produces a situation in which ideas, based solely on the logic of their own interrelationships, now lay claim to a kind of "higher reality" that can be far removed from the actual circumstances these ideas were originally intended to mirror.

As a result, our life can be determined by a type of logic that has little to do with the reality of human passion, enthusiasm or openness. Thus, Kierkegaard wrote in *The Present Age* (1962) that the process of abstraction "transforms the real task into an unreal trick and reality into a play" (p. 38). The consequences are destructive for our thinking and for our potential as human beings because abstraction is admirably suited for filtering out feelings. This makes abstraction itself an instrument of our destructiveness and especially of our *denied* destructiveness. If ideas are substituted for actual situations without regard for real motives and needs, we lose our access to these motives and needs, and our view of the world becomes a diminished and limited one without our necessarily being aware of this. But a diminished field of perception—although it may be considered scientific and bring us control and success in the short term—will inevitably have a destructive effect.

On the one hand, then, abstraction can lead to destructiveness; on the other, it can serve the denial of the destructiveness which builds up unavoidably in all of us and especially in those who are alienated from themselves and their feelings. A vicious circle results: the more our thinking is filled with abstractions, the less access we have to the reality of our emotional life and its destructive ramifications. We can, for instance, be advocates of "progress" without necessarily realizing that we may be sharing responsibility for the destruction of the environment or of other people. The logic of abstraction permits us to separate our personal involvement from the consequences of our position. After all, it's in the name of "progress" or "safeguarding peace," et cetera. Abstraction promotes depersonalization, the splitting off of embarrassing or painful feelings. And while society declares a goal such as progress worth striving for and brands everyone who questions it as suspect—as a betrayer of progress—the ideology behind it hides our split state. Thus, "reality" becomes a vicious game: what is actually done to people doesn't matter.

The ramifications can be seen on all sides. The oppression of women and the psychic impoverishment of men are prime examples, and yet we ascribe the resulting antagonism between the two sexes to "instincts." Actually, men see themselves and women *in terms of abstractions* in keeping with a philosophy that proclaims the necessity for strength, domination, and power rather than with the true reality of the other person. Fundamental to male behavior in our culture is the fear of helplessness, weakness, and vulnerability. The male cannot admit this fear to himself, for his philosophy preaches heroism. Even if heroism is not possible in his own case, it still remains his criterion of value. For this reason his self-esteem is based on the image of his importance (in other words, of his actual or even merely imagined power), for whose confirmation he requires admiration. And this is where the abstraction of "woman" comes to his aid, for she, in her supposed inferiority or at least lower station, is assigned the task of building up and stabilizing his self-image by recognizing his "strength" and "higher station."

We can learn a great deal about the effect of these abstract concepts governing our actions from those women who do *not* go along with them. In his novel *The Rainbow* (1949), written in 1915, D. H. Lawrence paints the portrait of such a woman in the person of the young teacher Winifred Inger, who says:

> The men fuss and talk, but they are really inane. They make everything fit into an old, inert idea. Love is a dead idea to them. They don't come to one and love one, they come to an idea, and they say "You are my idea," so they can embrace themselves. As if I were any man's idea! As if I exist because a man has an idea of me! As if I will be betrayed by him, lend him my body as an instrument for his idea, to be a mere apparatus of his dead theory. . . . They can't *take* a woman. They come to their own idea every time, and take that. They are like serpents trying to swallow themselves because they are hungry. (p. 343)

Abstraction makes us men unreal and the love we search for so frantically remains beyond our grasp. Instead of seeking true intimacy, we crave admiration from a woman. The product of the resultant mutual affirmation of self-images is called reality. But this way neither man nor woman actually touches the other; we remain invulnerable but, unfortunately, empty and unfulfilled as well. And this emptiness produces fear, fear rage, and rage aggression, forcing us further and further into a form of abstract behavior that only intensifies the splitting off of feelings.

Many women cooperate in this game by taking the image of the man's power at face value. They accept his views, on the one hand, by granting him the affirmation he seeks and, on the other, by thereby exercising "power" themselves. For the woman sex can then become the way of possessing the man and attaining his mythologized powers. That this is an act of destructiveness and not of love is evident from the covert revenge taken by those women who are determined to take charge of a man's fate: they force him always and in every situation to be a "hero."

In his novel *Women in Love* (1960), written in 1920, D. H. Lawrence again illustrates this situation with the figure of Gudrun and her relationship with Gerald, the powerful industrialist:

> . . . She kissed him, though her passion was a transcendent fear of the thing he was, touching his face with her infinitely delicate, encroaching, wondering fingers. Her fingers went over the mould of his face, over his features. How perfect and foreign he was—ah, how dangerous! . . . She kissed him, putting her fingers over his face, his eyes, his nostrils . . . to know him, to gather him in by touch. . . . He was an unutterable enemy, yet glistening with uncanny white fire. . . . Ah, if she could have the precious *knowledge* of him, she would be filled, and nothing could deprive her of this. . . . Her fingers had him under their power. The fathomless, fathomless desire they could evoke in him was deeper than death, where he had no choice. (p. 374)

Lawrence knew that such women—exactly like the men whose creations they are—do not see members of the opposite sex as individuals but as abstractions of power which they have to possess. It is fascinating to read his description of Gudrun's caresses, which are quickened by hatred but sexually arousing; he shows a keen perception of that unconscious love for what is deadly, a love that originates in the infant's dependency on a cold and/or rejecting love object—his mother.

Historical Development

Paradoxically, it is the course of development of science itself that has lent support to this situation. An intellectual climate was created in which the assumption prevailed that the reality of the world could be described perfectly by means of abstract concepts alone, since these had been so successful in the evolution of science. In this climate the intellectual process of abstraction was so generalized and glorified that any doubts or questions concerning its validity were seen as tantamount to a lack of loyalty to the ideal of human progress (see Whitehead 1925). The scientific worldview that began its rise in the seventeenth century simply assumed that all reality could be described by its methods. Whatever could not be accommodated by this approach, such as our moral nature and our existential consciousness, was simply excluded from "scientific" observation. In 1927 the English mathematician J. W. N. Sullivan pointed out in *Beethoven* (1960) that science remained "perpetually within its own domain by the device of cyclic definition," creating a mental climate that allowed "only certain growths to come to maturity, stunting and warping all others" (p. 14). Thus, a split between intelligence and feeling received cultural sanction.

The resultant invalidation of the world of feeling is still with us and keeps more and more people from using their intelligence as a tool to bring to light their deepest emotional experiences. Particularly in the social sciences—in spite of their apparent concern for the contents of our experience—the process of abstraction as a means of separating us from ourselves is being increasingly institutionalized. On the pretext that their methodology cannot adequately deal with human experience, they simply abolish it. In *The Measure of Man* (1962), Joseph Wood Krutch had this to say: ". . . To observe human or animal behavior *as though* it were merely mechanical, is inevitably to make it seem so; . . . to begin with the proposition 'We cannot conveniently deal with consciousness and therefore we are justified in disregarding it,' is simply to invite the confusions which have in actual fact arisen. It is to assume that what a given method finds intractable simply does not exist" (p. 164).

In the social sciences the primacy of methodology has brought about the identification of method with science itself. The limits imposed by such a methodology reflect uncritically the parameters of a definition that stipulates what may and may not be regarded as scientific. Whatever in human experience cannot be accommodated by a specific methodology is then declared invalid: it doesn't exist.

Thus, a lapidary fiat reduces the dimensions of our experience; consequently, it is no wonder that a B. F. Skinner (1971) can simplify them into a matter of "input" and "output," without leaving any room for freedom and dignity. The irony is that this sort of simplification and reduction of human experience creates its own validity. By defining in advance what is relevant, we no longer need to concern ourselves with what actually occurs. For it is in fact possible to perceive human beings and animals in terms of reduction to their behavioral patterns and to predict this behavior "scientifically," as Kavanau's research, referred to above, demonstrates. What in reality are attempts at autonomy become "errors" in the eyes of a scientist like Skinner. The method predetermines the result!

In this connection it is interesting to see how the Danish author Baroness Karen Blixen (under the pseudonym Isak Dinesen), in her autobiographical book *Out of Africa* (1937), describes a German scientist who complained to her about the "primitive" African natives he was using as subjects in an experiment. For the sake of the validity of his results, he wanted to systematize their behavior, but they strongly resisted any standardization. They acted exactly like the mice in Kavanau's experiment: they reacted with "incorrect" behavior in order to introduce some variation into an otherwise unbearably monotonous world of scientific research. Their behavior was full of "errors," and from the perspective of the German scientist they were "stupid." Blixen came to the following conclusion: "I sometimes thought that what, at the bottom of their hearts, they feared from us was pedantry. In the hands of a pedant they die of grief" (p. 24).

A scientist of completely different bent, the Nobel Prize winner George Wald, once reported on an encounter (1969), both characteristic and distressing, he had with a Harvard colleague from the psychology department: "One day he said to me, his face just shining, 'Give us the specifications, and we'll make the men.' I'm afraid I lost control a little, and my first reply was, 'Not if I can shoot you first.' That seemed to irritate him." (Professor Skinner and his laboratory are also located at Harvard.)

The view of life implicit in the social sciences today, in addition to being in danger of no longer corresponding to our common human experience, is also making it difficult for us to recognize ourselves, for a socially acceptable approach is dominant in these disciplines. The discrepancy between what is officially acceptable as experience and what we actually experience is blocking access to our feelings.

An Example

Let us look at Latané and Darley's often-cited experiment in the field of social psychology, which was awarded the 1968 prize for that discipline by the American Association for the Advancement of Science. I draw attention to this particular experiment on account of the prestigious and important award involved, for this sort of recognition throws light on the spirit of official psychology, a spirit which—in spite of all its rhetoric about the advancement of human progress—actually appears to legitimatize splitting-off, alienation, and dehumanization.

The occasion for this research project on bystander apathy was the murder of the social worker Kitty Genovese on a March night in 1964 in Queens, New York, by a mentally disturbed attacker. At least thirty-eight of her neighbors looked on without one of them coming to the wounded woman's aid or—although the murderer took over half an hour to finish his deed—even calling the police.

The researchers did not believe that apathy, indifference, moral callousness, dehumanization, or loss of concern for one's fellow human beings could be at the bottom of this awful event. If anything, they refer with disdain to "preachers, professors, and other sermonizers" who see a moral flaw in this failure to help a person in mortal terror and distress. They define the "real" dimensions of what happened by stating that "there are few positive rewards for success-ful action in an emergency. . . . Faced with a situation in which there is no benefit to be gained . . . it is perhaps surprising that anyone should intervene at all."

By assuming that we function like machines in keeping with the scheme of input/output and immediate concrete rewards (financial reward or status enhancement), the authors are unable to recognize dimensions that transcend such modes of behavior. The transcendental realm disappears completely, and the facts of human experience are distorted by means of denial. People respond spontaneously to terror and to the distress of others, since we all have a predisposition toward empathy and sympathy. And those who have the greatest access to themselves in this area of experience cannot live with the denial of that tendency. Apparently, however, these two researchers can, making it possible for them to devise complexly organized experimental situations for testing the relationship between the chance presence of bystanders and the degree to which one individual reacts to the distress of another. Their findings, so they maintain, indicate that people are less ready to offer assistance when other onlookers are present.

Their method of investigation places primary emphasis on the varying distance between the spectator and the person in distress; in this case we of course can "see" and "measure" the distance involved. What is lost sight of in the procedure is the transcendent realm of inner experience and the question of how and why human beings choose to shun the voice of their own humanity. But since all that counts in this method is what is measurable, nothing appears to be lost sight of! A purely mechanical element—the space between the people present—provides the framework for the experiment, and everything else is then nonexistent. The measurements involved yield data that can be processed mathematically. Thus, our consciousness is seen to be dominated by strictly *external* factors and an entire *internal* world disappears.

Let us look now at several significant findings that were simply ignored by the researchers. For instance, their tables reveal that a considerable number of people in the experiment did come to the victim's aid, but since their behavior deviated from that of the majority, it was declared insignificant by means of statistical methods. Because Latané and Darley didn't consider such human reactions as statistically relevant, they simply disregarded them. It is the *method* that determines which facts are admissible, not *reality*. Perhaps even more important is that a large number of those who didn't come to the victim's assistance (in other words, those upon whom the researchers based their statistical "proof") exhibited strong psychosomatic symptoms. I quote: "Many of these subjects showed physical signs of nervousness; they often had trembling hands and sweating palms" (p. 264).

What do we learn from this behavior, which, although noted by the authors, was then passed over? It clearly illustrates that people who ignore the promptings of their own humanity when faced with another's distress cannot escape the somatic results of their betrayal of a fellow human being. Milgram's experiment discussed in chapter 1 has already shown that when we shun the voice of our own humanity and suppress our empathic reactions, they will be expressed in body language in the form of psychosomatic symptoms. Although the researchers in the case of Kitty Genovese do inform us of these symptoms, they overlook their significance because for ideological reasons they are interested in playing down the role of our emotional experience. By so doing, they are helping to intensify the prevailing violence and aggression in our society.

When we are confronted with the helplessness of another person but turn our back on it because we repudiate it in ourself, that person arouses our self-hatred. Faced with helplessness, our fear is transformed into anger at the victim for serving as a mirror of our own hated self. What we are doing is making the victim responsible for our own "weakness." This is the revenge we take for our own repressed humiliation, a mechanism with a long history of development. Here we find the underlying reason for our identification with violence, an identification that scientists like Latané and Darley not only conceal but reinforce through their concealment. They make it difficult for us to discover that the actual source of our cruelty and callousness lies in the rejection of our own suffering. The more inhumanly we behave, the more we repudiate our suffering and betray that human self we were never permitted to have.

What Latané and Darley are unable to inform us about and what they cover over with a cloak of denial, whether consciously or not, is *why* it is that people become hard-hearted; furthermore, they deny the possibility of feeling aversion toward brutal behavior. Mainstream psychology here uses scientific arguments to conceal human perversity. Even Rudolf Höss, the dreaded commandant of the death camp of Auschwitz, could not fully escape all remnants of human feelings. He reports a nervous breakdown he suffered when these feelings threatened to break through his robotlike state (*The Autobiography of Rudolf Höss*, 1959; see also Kempinski, 1973).

Yet the modern social sciences are in the process of making perversity acceptable. Thus, the authors in question can present us with the following conclusion: "[When] several observers are present . . . the responsibility for intervention is shared among all the onlookers. . . . As a result, each may be less likely to help. . . . [Situational factors involving the immediate social environment are seen to be] of greater importance in determining an individual's reaction than such vague cultural or personality concepts as 'apathy' or 'alienation due to urbanization'. . . . The failure to intervene may be better understood by knowing the relationship among bystanders rather than between a bystander and the victim."

Hatred, Self-Hatred, and Evil as Flight from the Self

In denying that the crucial issue is the relationship of bystander to victim, Latané and Darley sanction the *escape of the self into a group* and thereby alter our very conception of reality. Their elimination of the tension between what is and what ought to be (as Herbert Marcuse put it in 1964) establishes a new reality that subverts essential features of our experience and justifies our hiding behind a group. The fact that somatic symptoms furnish proof of the presence of shame, guilt, cowardice, and other suppressed feelings is simply overlooked. Objectivity, accuracy, and "scientific" procedure are perverted in order to discredit or distort human experience. While our patients are suffering because they are unable to live authentic lives, these propagandists of dissociation and a split state insist upon a falsified picture of reality which denies the validity of suffering.

What this type of modern scientist promotes as the norm of human behavior is at bottom dangerous madness. Norms such as these conceal the causes of our traumas and our vulnerability; a diminished, perverted humanity is locked into a clever system whose aim it is to foist upon us a society in which a universal consensus will protect us from self-doubt, fear, and anxieties. But the attempt fails, for we are inoculated with a new disease. Under the guise of being concerned with feelings, this new "scientific" society in actuality repudiates them. Since our access to them is therefore blocked, we experience the malady of callousness to a heightened degree. And such lack of feeling always entails intensified anger and aggression.

To the extent to which our true self is lost and our human sympathies and the responsibility for them disappear, we become vengeful without even being able to realize it. The aggression is a reaction to a decrease in autonomy, even in those cases where a person tries to struggle against this loss. The whole history of our childhood is repeated here; parental suppression of the child's feelings and spontaneous responses succeeds in making the child obedient, but that only conceals and at the same time intensifies the aggression. The child's rage is directed against its own suffering and sense of aliveness, for these are apparently what caused the parents' oppressive behavior in the first place. The first split in our being is the result: the rejection of what could have become the foundation for the development of our autonomy—namely, our sense of aliveness. And although we have been made accomplices in our own suppression, this doesn't mean that our self-hatred is diminished as a consequence; on the contrary, a continual process of splitting off takes place, which is reinforced by societal norms.

The source of aggression and destructiveness lies in our culture, not in the individual. And everything that reinforces the fragmentation of our personality and closes off access to our inner world contributes to the creation and growth of our destructive drives. The truly impaired in our culture are not the mentally ill, the psychiatric patients who are shunned by society; they are the people who want to impose upon us a belief in a diminished human reality. Those who are ill unconsciously point out to us the path back to ourself; the others close off this path with their pseudoconvincing and pseudoexonerative theoretical constructs.

If our refusal to come to the aid of a fellow human being is translated into terms of a purely geometric relationship between bystanders and victim, the ability to maintain our own integrity will be shattered. When that occurs, there are only two possibilities: either we will feel so uneasy and unwell that we will suffer a breakdown, or we will have to destroy what awakens our uneasiness. In the latter case, the inevitable consequences are cruelty and sadism. Every police system built on cruelty and every system of torture is shaped by that inner logic which forces its functionaries to be in constant flight from themselves. They attempt to escape by becoming increasingly cruel to their victims. Only when the victim no longer cries out and the torturer can then leave his own perpetually denied pain behind him does the torture stop.

The violence and destructiveness I am describing here need not be a personal matter nor physical in a direct sense. It is not always easy to recognize in what situations and to what extent we are being cut off from our feelings. But such a phenomenon constitutes murder—even though in installments—of our self. The research project on bystander apathy just discussed is, in conception and in its actual influence, violent and destructive. Tacitly, it grants legitimacy to the merging of the self with the group by translating this occurrence into operational, geometric terms, thereby precipitating the downfall of our ability to think, to respond to reality, and to behave morally, as well as to pass moral judgments.

The Diminished Self

People with a dimension of inner experience that belies the official jargon are in danger, since they deviate from the norm, of being classified as mentally handicapped or disturbed. It is diminished human beings who are presented to us as normal. These are the people who cope most successfully (and apparently without problems) with a diminished world.

In our daily dealings with people who function "better" in this diminished world than we do, we may even feel inferior on occasion. In his *Sketchbook 1966–1971* (1974), the Swiss writer Max Frisch reports a conversation he had with a painter and decorator—and with his description opens our eyes to this shrunken form of human existence.

The two men are sitting across from each other in a restaurant, and the author gets the other man to talk as they eat. The painter has six men working for him, and the talk is about pay rates for night work, spray techniques, sports, et cetera.

I finally get to the point: Which work do you like best? I would rather paint a wall than window frames, bright colors rather than dull matching tones. Why is that? He doesn't understand the question. Which does he prefer dealing with, redecorated or new buildings? One just does both—tonight redecorating. Does he dislike night work? One just has to put up with it. Since he is the boss and can therefore select, I ask: Which part of the work do you keep for yourself? Undercoating must be boring enough, but removing old paint even worse. Which gives you more pleasure, using a brush or spraying? His specialty, he says, is hard finishing: that's where the profit lies. So back to the current rates. . . . Back to my question: What in your work do you occasionally enjoy doing? His answers: Spraying is more profitable, redecorations bring in very little, the rates for windows are much too low, on the other hand he does well from hard finishing, and after all he has a family to support, night work is profitable. My further question: Doesn't it annoy you when people choose colors that you personally find wrong? I know, of course, that he is simply working for a living, but all the same I ask my question: Wouldn't you sometimes like to select a different color? One tries out patterns in the hall and then can be amazed with the finished result: doesn't he look forward to seeing how it will turn out? He doesn't really understand what I am trying to get at; he has told me his income. Don't you sometimes feel like taking up another profession? Well, of course: when a job doesn't pay because of the low rates (with the exception of lacquering, which is his specialty), then his income goes down. Do you get a kick out of lacquering? He wouldn't exactly say that: hard finishing is a job. . . . He must go now, which he does, not offering his hand, morosely*. . . . (Pp. 35–36)

It is already clear that abstract concepts diminish our spontaneous expressions of aliveness. But the question arises just how far our world of scientific specialization, the whole scientific establishment, is—perhaps involuntarily—practicing and insisting on acceptance for this reduced way of living.

Outsiders and Failures

Again and again it is the artists and outsiders who liberate our thinking from the reductive views of official ideologies. *The Outsider* (1956), Colin Wilson's study of outsiders in the areas of

*Author's translation.

literature, painting, and the dance, interprets their creative accomplishments as a struggle against the bonds of a culture that diminishes the individual. The interesting thing is that this same culture generally claims later that their successes are attributable to its encouragement. But in each case it is the attempt not to allow the culture to split them off from their personal world of feelings that enabled these artists (and outsiders) to develop their self-rooted talents in the first place.

Wilson sees their struggle as one for their own truth, which is undoubtedly accurate. But on the deepest level it is a battle to maintain their integrity and remain whole, to keep from being split in those areas where the culture demands such diminishment. (Of course the artist may be split in other areas.) And the culture continually demands this, especially where it has impaired our autonomy so that we will not become aware of the sources of our aggression and destructiveness.

When we are crushed in our struggle for wholeness and autonomy by the pressure of official distortions, often the only outlet that remains to us for expressing our autonomy is mentally disturbed behavior. Charlotte Perkins Gilman, in a brilliant and moving short story, "The Yellow Wallpaper" (originally published in 1892), portrays a woman's lonely and futile fight against the fragmentation of her emotions. She is at the mercy of her husband's greed for possession, which is officially interpreted as love and concern for her. The only path leading out of her life-threatening situation—the wife herself is imprisoned in her "good" husband's abstractions and can't defend herself directly—is by the destruction of all rationally constructed types of relationships. And so the woman becomes schizophrenic before our very eyes. (Hardly ever in the medical literature will we find a more convincing description of the onset of schizophrenia than in the thirty-seven pages of Gilman's story.)

The schizophrenic presents us with a picture of exaggerated helplessness in which we may recognize the repudiated childhood helplessness we no longer have access to. So painful is our memory of being at the mercy of the parental will that first we have had to split it off and then repress it. Later, we are exposed to a culture that equates helplessness with weakness and offers us power and domination as the means of escape from feelings of anxiety and despair. And so we have learned to run away from the experience of helplessness; if we don't, we become "failures." Thus, almost all of us dream of success, of conquests, of powerful deeds in order to escape our feelings of helplessness, anxiety, and despair. But these feelings will catch up with us in our childhood nightmares—and later as well!

The abstractions we accept as valid parameters for our existence increase our inner malaise and urge toward violence, for they cut us off from the feelings helplessness produces in us. The only means by which we can manage to come to terms with our repudiated helplessness are insane ones, which, however, are split off from any consciousness of their insanity.

For how else are we to interpret the megalomania of those people who flee their helplessness by dreaming of world conquest, mass murder, battles, and superhuman successes? We fail to notice that behind these delusions of grandeur is rejection of the experience of helplessness. The abstraction blocking our path to this realization is the view which regards despair as weakness, a judgment all of us are secretly shamed by. We fear a weakness that exists only thanks to an abstraction!

That is why we are never able to make the discovery that if we only accept our powerlessness, we will not die of it. The concept of weakness makes such a discovery impossible. Our fear of being a failure drives us to make ever greater demands on ourselves or else causes us to have a permanent feeling of being cheated and inferior, all of which then keeps us in a constant state of inner tension and anger. Moreover, this state of impotence is the driving force behind our perpetual search for an identity not our own (in other words, a nonautonomous one) and is thus a source of inexhaustible rage. We can neither conquer nor recognize our rage since the abstractions determining our life's parameters keep us at a distance from our true feelings; we seek reasons for it but only in our victims, not in our own reality, for we fail to realize that we ourselves are the original victims. We therefore take our revenge on what we regard as weakness in others, which in reality is the weakness we reject and hate in ourselves. Hatred for Jews is a striking example of this phenomenon.

Another example, illustrating with its ghostlike unreality the same phenomenon, comes from the first years of the economic recession that occurred under President Nixon. Some of the unemployed were interviewed in Spokane, Washington—most of them engineers who had lost their jobs due to economic setbacks in the aerospace industry. While waiting to collect their unemployment checks, they were asked what they saw as the greatest problem at the moment. Almost all responded that it was the problem of busing, the transportation of black pupils to schools in white areas of the city!

We seek alien victims rather than the real source of our rage, since we cannot recognize the truth and are unable to admit our own despair. And the more we express our rage, the more intense it becomes. If we don't discover its cause, our pathological state worsens and eventually produces a magical image of self and world. We feel invulnerable when we can victimize others, even torture them, without recognizing that it is our own helplessness that is being crushed.

What can be more magical and reinforce feelings of omnipotence more strongly than fantasies of mass destruction and conquest? In the guise of "sober" abstract concepts split off from feelings, they increase our ability to contemplate atrocities with equanimity. Such fantasies are now being played out daily in the form of computer "games" by men who consider themselves normal—good fathers, respectable professors, and the like.

What follows is one example of the modern war games played by elites throughout the so-called civilized world and considered to be normal mental exercises. In a "scholarly" article that appeared in the *Annals of the American Academy of Political and Social Science* (1970), Edmund O. Stillman—at the time director of the European division of the Hudson Institute and adviser to the U.S. Army and the Atomic Energy Commission—envisaged this scenario following a projected confrontation between the United States and China:

> The United States then announces the forthcoming destruction (within, say, 48 hours) of one of ten [Chinese] cities simultaneously announcing sanctuary areas. The announcement of ten likely cities is intended to augment the quality of terror and to drive large segments of the population into motion, disrupting or contributing to the disruption of governmental structure and authority. . . . In 48 hours the United States delivers a delayed-action warhead or bomb (set for 24 hours) in Mukden and simultaneously calls upon the Chinese people to overthrow the regime and save themselves. This attack is followed by similar attacks on three additional cities—Harbin, Changchow and Canton.

Here conceptualization, completely divorced from emotional reactions, leads to a thoroughly dispassionate contemplation of atrocity. These fantasies of destruction are on the same level as the power fantasies of the ideologues. Krylenko, head Soviet public prosecutor and later Commisar of Justice under Stalin, once said, according to Solzhenitsyn (1973), that people were not people but "carriers of specific ideas. [Therefore] no matter what the individual qualities [of the defendant] *only one* method of evaluating him is to be applied: evaluation from the point of view of class expedience."

The real issue, Solzhenitsyn ironically points out, is that some people consider the existence of others as inexpedient. But when the ideology of power shapes everyday citizens' views of reality, their autonomy disappears and abstraction reigns. This situation is illustrated by an item in the *New York Times* of July 3, 1970. Prior to a jury trial, the judge asked a prospective juror whether he considered the defendant guilty. The answer: "If he didn't do something, he wouldn't be here." (The defendant was a member of the Black Panther movement.) When the judge asked, "Suppose I had you arrested now?" the man replied, "That would mean I must have done something." A symptomatic line of reasoning! Here we see the complete surrender of individual autonomy, compensated for by a total identification with the ruling powers and their ideology.

Those who do not live in a world of abstractions are totally incapable of such a thing. It is abstraction that forces us to take revenge on victims who mirror our own oppression and evoke our self-hatred.

Clearly, ideological abstractions can cause murderers to be unaware of their own bloodthirstiness. The true motives for their behavior remain hidden, and they may even consider themselves peace loving. When cruelty is made an abstract concept, cruel acts are separated from the reality of feelings. It then becomes possible to subject others to cruel treatment without having to be aware of one's own emotional reaction of horror: the "body count" mentality of the Vietnam War and Nixon's use of the word "scenario" for actions that caused horrible suffering for untold numbers of human beings are aspects of this phenomenon. Abstractions estrange us from our feelings, which—if they are still present at all—tend to run in the direction of identification with the group, for then we need not take responsibility for them. It is in this connection that the approach of scholars like Latané and Darley and the hordes of their "scientific" disciples is so appalling—even criminal. A symptom of the degree to which perversity marks the official view of reality is the fact that people are described as unrealistic if they shudder at occurrences like the brutal murder in Queens and at the pseudoscientific attempts to explain the bystanders' reactions and deduce legitimate behavioral norms from them.

When people turn into robots because they see themselves in terms of abstract concepts, there is great danger of their unwittingly becoming evil. At the mercy of abstract conceptions of our existence that bear no relationship to our own reality, we will necessarily be filled with rage over this betrayal of the self, a rage that goes unnoticed. Although everyone deplores alcohol and drug abuse, aggressiveness, and sexual promiscuity, the connection is not made between these symptoms and the impairment of autonomy, for, again, abstractions based on a diminished view of humanity obstruct our vision. We would rather forgive the evil proliferating all around us than the rebellion against it, which we mistake for the true evil.

It is worth noting how many people believe that a certain dehumanization was the prerequisite for survival in the Nazi death camps, that one had to become primitive and asocial. Similarly, we recognize the "necessity" of becoming primitive in the case of wars and other catastrophes. In this same vein, we see the history of humankind in terms of progress from a state of barbarism to one of civilization. All these views are better suited to concealing the denial of our feelings than they are to revealing the truth.

Kempinski (1973), a Polish psychiatrist, and Pawelczyńska (1979), a sociologist, demonstrate that those who survived in concentration camps were the ones who refused to become brutish like their captors and held fast to their humanity. This is of course a finding that stands in complete contradiction to the theories of our "authorities" in the fields of psychology and psychiatry who have accorded a certain legitimacy to dehumanization. One of these authorities is Bruno Bettelheim (1958; 1961), even though he, more than others, undoubtedly understands a great deal about autonomy, as we can see from his brilliant work with autistic children!

The Survivor (1976) by Terrence Des Pres is a testimony to the human qualities that led to survival in the death camps. The author contends that the psychoanalytic method is misleading if it deals with behavior in the concentration camps as if it were symbolic and mediated behavior. Such an interpretation cannot be applied to actions in cases where life is characterized by extreme distress and desperation: ". . . when death itself is the determinant—then behavior has no 'meaning' at all in a symbolic or psychological sense" (p. 156). The survivor, according to Des Pres, was the person who, in accepting "the rule of death," was also the first for whom "Thou shalt not kill" became a commandment naturally obeyed. "There is a terrible irony in this, for whereas awareness of death generates firm care for life, death-denial ends in a fury of destruction." The survivor takes the opposite position from the one our culture forces on *us*, a culture in which "fear of death . . . can only be assuaged by insisting that life itself is worthless. The survivor is evidence that men and women are now strong enough, mature enough, awake enough, to face death without mediation, and therefore to embrace life without reserve" (pp. 206, 207).

Viktor Frankl's report (1968) of how he survived in a concentration camp is similar testimony to what is best in human beings. In the midst of a brutal and irreal reality he discovered human self-realization, experiencing an inner triumph by understanding that "man's inner strength may raise him above his outward fate" (p. 67). It was this fact, and not dehumanization, that made survival possible for him.

If our thinking is dictated by considerations of power alone, we will never be able to ask the question: what is the point of survival? Those who are manipulating the abstractions of politics, power, and domination simply assume that whatever results in survival must always be tantamount to the highest good. This line of reasoning represents a misunderstanding of Darwin's ideas, for according to his concept of the survival of the fittest, what is "fittest" may not necessarily be what is "best." The organisms best fitted to survive nuclear war are cockroaches—they will one day inherit our planet!

The process of abstraction repeats itself with increasingly fateful consequences. By separating us from our feelings, abstraction turns human beings into cripples. A person so crippled will inevitably seek, in Unamuno's words, "ominous relief in seeing mutilation all around him." He was responding to Franco's General Millan Astray's shout, "Long live death!" at a convocation of the University of Salamanca just at the beginning of the Civil War. (Payne 1962).

But abstraction can bring about mutilation by means other than physical force. Society can exert force not only by directly suppressing the development of autonomy but also by stressing values and orientations that leave no room for it.

The present-day emphasis in education on cognitive performance illustrates this. Bruner, Oliver, Greenfield, et. al. (1966)
were in the forefront of those pedagogic psychologists who
measure intellectual growth by the ability to handle and master
abstractions at an early age. Success at cognitive tasks thus
becomes a socially desirable goal. Proficiency in dealing with
abstractions in early childhood initiates a process that will later
enable the child to climb the ladder of advancement and success.
Ironically, a child who adapts effortlessly to this process is classified as *independent*, independence in this context being syn-
onomous with success and material wealth. But it is precisely the
kind of effort and skill involved here that blocks off those areas of
children's emotional life—joy, sorrow, high spirits, and despair—
which form the only basis for true independence or autonomy.
These emotions provide the bridge to a child's own perceptions.
The "independent," "successful" child, however, will have no time
for them, since they interfere with the mastery of cognitive skills.

Similarly, performance-oriented child rearing precludes the
type of maternal care that makes it possible for a child to develop
in an emotionally integrated way. A relatively recent study of
maternal care and its effects on cognitive performance (Wieder
1972) clearly demonstrates that patterns of maternal behavior
considered to be "good" (i.e., nonpunitive manipulation that
enables an infant to eat solid foods, feed itself, and become toilet
trained early on) show a positive correlation with cognitive
performance as early as the eighteenth and twenty-second
months. What is really involved here is a kind of mothering that
manipulates the child through the use of rewards. It is a method
that may satisfy the mother's ambition, but it is not an expression
of delight in her child's vitality. This approach equates success in
the cognitive field (for instance, command of mathematical skills)
with progress in personal development. In other words, those
patterns of maternal behavior that encourage pseudo-indepen-
dence in a child—yet actually prevent authentic autonomy—
produce high cognitive achievement.

In her book *Prisoners of Childhood* (1981), Alice Miller gives a powerful and empathic description of the way a child's self is suppressed for the sake of "success"; she does not distinguish, however, between a form of adaptation that permits inner rebellion and one that gives birth to evil. This is probably because she fails to differentiate between real suffering and suffering that is a type of maneuver. In her second book, *For Your Own Good* (1983), she sees Hitler and Christiane F. as suffering personalities. But they are not people who suffer because they are sensitive; on the contrary, they exemplify the category of pseudoaffectivity summed up by Helene Deutsch (1934, 1942) in the phrase "as if" and resemble those psychopaths studied by Cleckley (1964). To try to explain away evil in therapeutic language diminishes reality.

The most destructive aspect of the form of child rearing just described is that children who are constantly subjected to pedagogic compulsion, applied without overt punishment, are incapable of recognizing their anger at being manipulated through the use of rewards. They have a deep sense of dissatisfaction, whose source, however, remains hidden from them. The modern school of psychology responsible for this approach produces people who are under the sway of a rage of which they are not conscious. The strong effort to achieve, which gives structure to their life, is an expression of this unrecognized rage. The drive motivating these people is a destructive one, but its effects are (or can be) camouflaged under the guise of achievement. There is no need for them to acknowledge their true motivation, for abstraction fragments their field of vision.

Henry T. Nash (1980), a professor of political science, has described adults who are products of this kind of upbringing. Once a Department of Defense analyst, he characterizes his former colleagues as "people whose speech and behavior suggest their sociability. . . . Nothing in the air seems sinister or hints of guilt." Yet, using a camouflaged language whose abstract concepts fragment reality, these kindhearted people can "plan to incinerate vast numbers of unknown human beings without any sense of moral revulsion."

We "see" ourselves in terms of concepts that do not correspond to our real nature. The urgent task of present-day psychotherapy must be to reduce this dissociation which is threatening us with annihilation. People try to hide within a group, where they can deny their rage and destructiveness. They have learned to assume a social image for themselves, but deep inside they long to take revenge for the suppression of their autonomy. Essentially, what they have learned—often completely unconsciously—is that coexistence is not possible, although this knowledge contradicts social norms (the ideology of pluralism). "There is no co-existence, one must either yield or win"; that is the basic experience when autonomy is destroyed. People who have been cripped as a result of their "adaptation" to this situation will use the socially sanctioned striving for success and achievement as their form of revenge. Nowadays, destructiveness on a monstrous scale does not have to manifest itself in the form of a Genghis Khan or an Adolf Hitler; it often appears as goodness, a smiling face, or progress.

The German writer Hugo Ball (1919) once wrote, "Knowledge, when it appears as the highest principle, necessarily kills enthusiasm, kills the spirit." Albert Szent-Györgyi (1964) put it in more personal terms: "I do not depreciate knowledge"; what schools need to do "is to make us learn how to learn, to whet our appetites for knowledge, to teach us the delight of doing a job well and the excitement of creativity, to teach us to love what we do, and to help us find what we love to do."

It is certainly no accident that young, over-intellectual patients in psychotherapy are often unable to verbalize their real feelings. Their talents have been directed exclusively toward one goal: to be as well prepared as possible for competing in the "cognitive area." For this reason, it has become impossible for them to carry on a dialogue with themselves.

The case of a young woman who entered analysis exemplifies this situation: her body began to tremble violently every time she had to go along with the social game requiring everyone in the group to be nice and to feel virtuous in their togetherness. This was expected, for example, in the research laboratory where she worked; that way, everyone would reinforce the accepted image of being a nice, cooperative colleague to work with. But in the course of her therapy, the patient became aware that she was experiencing conflicting impressions; she sensed, for instance, contempt on the part of the person who dominated the group. Not only were her impressions not shared by the group, but the myth of solidarity caused the others to turn against anybody who questioned this fiction. The patient was having difficulty in therapy because she could not verbalize what she was feeling with such intensity, for she possessed no verbal "tools." She had been molded in childhood by models of togetherness and solidarity; there was no place in her family mythology for the conflicts and contradictions that occur in real life. Everything her parents did for her was always an expression of their "well-meaning" concern.

Her trembling was part of a "copping out" in which feeling like a failure was an aspect of her struggle not to lead a false life. Still, she was incapable of admitting to herself that she had been insulted, for example; the abstract mode of behavior of which she was a captive didn't permit such a thing. It was her body, then, that had to speak for her.

In her book *Teacher* (1963), Sylvia Ashton-Warner, a remarkable elementary school teacher, writes about encountering a similar inability to verbalize in her pupils in New Zealand. In her work with Maori children who had been educated according to the value system of Western culture, she discovered that they either denied their inner fears or couldn't recognize them. These fears found expression in destructive behavior. "I'm not afraid of anything," one of her pupils cried; when she asked if he wasn't perhaps afraid after all, he replied, "No, I stick my knife into it all!" (pp. 36, 38). When she succeeded in giving her pupils the words with which they could gain access to their fears, they gave up their destructive behavior. As their destructive urge disappeared, it was replaced by creativity and positive learning.

The interesting point here is that when abstractions blocked these children's access to their feelings, the resulting aggression was expressed openly. This was so because success and performance and camouflaging of aggression had not yet become the central concern of their lives as they have for us in the West.

I once read aloud a chapter from Henry Miller's auto-biographical work *Black Spring* (1963) to a psychotherapy seminar at Rutgers University. The chapter deals with a family gathering that took place when Miller was around twelve.

Food, alcohol, and good cheer abounded, but under the surface the family members were all interested in stabbing one another in the back. Only Miller's Tante Melia had a heart, but she was losing her mind. On this of all days his family had given Henry the task of taking his aunt to a state-run mental home; they wanted to get rid of her without having to pay for it. And this took place while everyone was "merry and bright." When Henry said goodbye to her in front of the gate to the asylum, he cried; she had always trusted him:

> Even though she was a half-wit she was good to me. The others were more intelligent, but their hearts were bad. . . . When Mele stood at the gate with eyes so round and bright her mind must have traveled back like an express train. Everything must have leaped to her mind at once. Her eyes were so big and bright, as if they saw more than they could comprehend. Bright with terror, and beneath the terror a limitless confusion. That's what made them so beautifully bright. You have to be crazy to see things so lucidly, so all at once. (Pp. 108, 111)

I asked the members of the seminar to write down what they thought Miller's feelings had been. Only one of them, a student from Mexico, wrote about Miller's despair; the others handed in sociological diagrams of family constellations and their interactions. No one, except for this young man, was able to deal with the reality of a despairing situation. I was aghast. Was there any possibility at all of teaching people who were so estranged from themselves anything about their own selves? I came to the next lecture resolved to let them know my opinion. "Oh," they chorused almost with one voice, "you wanted us to write something *simple,* about feelings!"

I told this story to Henry Miller. He burst out laughing at the absurdity of an education that estranges people from life by rewarding only abstractions and "complexity." These young people were schooled not to react feelingly to their experiences but rather to distance themselves from them. Abstraction makes this possible. The course of their life was determined by their ability to manipulate abstract formulae (e.g., family constellations) in a virtuoso manner; this ability is the criterion of their future success. Since success furnishes an opportunity, as well as an excuse, for being ruthless, they end by practicing a socially approved form of aggression.

David Harris, who spent time in prison as victim of post-McCarthyism, writes in his book *Goliath* (1970) about those "institutionalized abstractions" that produce people whose actions bear no relation at all to their real needs. What people take to be their own feelings is merely what society requires them to feel. Harris says, "When our doing is not an immediate process of making ourselves real (when the object and the intention of an act are not realized in the act itself), a direct relationship to ourselves is impossible. . . . Soldiers make war in the pursuit of peace. . . . The intention of the act is in no way carried in the act itself" (pp. 59, 62). (Harris's former wife, folk singer Joan Baez, reports that he always insisted on looking at the world through the windows of his own soul.)

All that remains then is an identity that can be assembled like something on a production line according to rules established by the abstractions of a given society. If we reject the rules, we risk becoming outcasts, which may then weaken us to such an extent that our very existence is jeopardized.

The force of the abstractions shaping us is directed against our authenticity. Abstraction—as an environment that clouds our vision and as a process that absolves us of our emotional responsibility for life—turns into the enemy of life itself. Our intelligence then becomes a power that transforms reality into a dangerous self-destructive game. Those who attempt to break out of this system—by not surrendering to it—are labelled as maladjusted and as failures. As long ago as the thirteenth century, one of these "maladjusted" spirits, Meister Eckhart, wrote—under circumstances similar to today's: "When I preached at Paris, I said—and I regard it as well said—that with all their science, those people at Paris are not able to discern what God is in the least of creatures—not even in a fly" (Blackney 1941).

III

The Dehumanization of Men and the Oppression of Women

The Hunger for Power

THE hunger for power destroys a man's soul. In his blind pursuit of it he diminishes himself, as well as the woman whom he needs to confirm his image of being powerful. It is this image which—consciously or unconsciously—has come to be identified with his sense of being. In this context there is no possibility of genuine love, for only what validates the image will be admissible within a relationship. The self that one could have been is hated because it revolved around the experience of helplessness and suffering. Genuine commitment, genuine knowledge of the other person and oneself are avoided. One lives charades; and if these do not function, one becomes furious and murderous.

We are constantly searching for heroes (or heroines), and when the one we have chosen turns out to be a real person, we abandon him (or her). We despise the person ever after, never noticing that, in keeping with the logic of this pattern, the "loss" makes us feel weakened and near death. The undercurrents of depression and despair beneath the glittering surface of our culture are unmistakable signs of this.

As men, we glorify the woman who is obliging and tries to please us, without ever realizing that the price we must pay is inevitable disappointment and wounded feelings. We want warmth from women, but at the same time we fear it. This is why we content ourselves with a sham: *we allow ourselves to be driven to seek greatness.* Instead of providing security, warmth and mutual support, the relationship to woman becomes the source for unending fantasies of grandiosity and secret claims to superiority. The stratagem of a counterfeit love displaces a genuine one; we need not be afraid now of becoming a prisoner of our need for love. Women are also caught up in this game and play along with us. I am thinking of someone like Alma Schindler (Mahler), who attempted to find self-fulfillment through Gustav Mahler, Walter Gropius, Oskar Kokoschka, and Franz Werfel. The sad thing is that her efforts were unnecessary, since she had sufficient strength of her own.

It is in the image of strength, decisiveness, power, fearlessness, knowledge, and control—an image free of feelings of anxiety or guilt—that a man locates his "personality." Only by developing this image can he gain a sense of himself. It is not what he really feels or might feel that is crucial for him but an image—that is, an abstraction, a metaphysical idea of heroism—whose logic and frame of reference motivate him. It is this way of thinking, ultimately dedicated to making us avoid reality, that guides us.

What is the nature of the reality he flees? A world full of emotions, permeated with the experience of inadequacy, helplessness, pain, despair, and fear of failure; a world in which feelings of impotence and rage are present but must constantly be translated into a sense of being invulnerable and unassailable. True, not all of us—and not all who admit to having such feelings—let our behavior be guided by them. But what would happen if we (no doubt the majority of us) could admit how easily we can feel held in contempt and insulted!

Naturally, the reality of the world of genuine emotions includes other experiences as well: joy, ecstasy, courage, grief. But I am not referring to the kind of joy that emerges when one has put something over on someone, or the ecstasy that can come from successful competition, that is, all those experiences that are the function of an *"imposed"* reality: the necessity to be successful in order to *escape* failure. I am speaking here of a joy based on empathy: or the joy of taking pleasure in the growth and development of another—even of a plant; the sharing of joy as well as sorrow. And it is this type of experience which leads to a strength that does *not* depend on constantly having to prove oneself. The latter is only the mirror image of the fear of being a failure! We struggle to avoid failure and are not even aware that our fear of failure drives us into a nightmare of "strength." On the other hand, the strength that grows out of sorrow, distress, helplessness, illness, and bitter pain has to do with the kind of transcendent experience that brings *inner* fortitude, which is not contingent upon external power and its constant need for reaffirmation.

Thus, it is our compulsion to fit an image of power which keeps us from experiencing the reality that is—with devastating consequences! We establish irrational ideals of the "real" man and the "right kind" of woman, which not only separate us more and more from our genuine potentialities but in the long run also lead us into self-destructiveness.

The Ituri of the rain forests of the Congo (Turnbull 1962) do not conform to metaphysical models of being. They are aware that such models exist, to be sure, but they make fun of them. As a result, there are no differences in sensitivity between the sexes. Tenderness, joy, sorrow, all emotions are shared and expressed equally. And, as the English anthropologist Geoffrey Gorer (1966) has pointed out, since Ituri men are not concerned with metaphysical concepts of "masculinity," by means of which they prove themselves and compare themselves with other men, there seems to be none of the homosexuality in their culture that is always latent in ours. In our society, every man has suspicions about himself and must prove to himself that he is not homosexual—evidence of how pervasive are our doubts about our male adequacy. If it is unmanly to have tender feelings, then our own inclinations in this direction must be negated. By projecting these feelings onto another man, we can now negate them in ourselves and attack them in him.

In this way, an abstract system determines our life, our relationships, the violence of our behavior, and, finally, the turn our violence takes toward self-destructiveness. This is something that is bound to occur, for the often unconscious feeling of impotence, which stems from the crippling of our genuine human potential, fills us with rage. Unaware of the source of this rage, we inevitably turn it against ourselves—or against the other person, who seems to be a reflection of our self.

Unfortunately, those people who best embody such ideals of masculinity become our leaders. Many women succumb to the same fascination for these ideals and thus force their male partner to adhere to them. Both of them fear what is inside themselves and punish with their contempt those whose search for the truth poses a threat. These attitudes can have a disastrous, even fatal effect, for the false definition of masculinity—often subscribed to by women, as I have said—leads to wars and to mercilessly competitive behavior, which may result in a heart attack, to mention just one form of self-destruction.

Men find themselves faced with a dilemma. They are afraid of women, who are nevertheless of great importance for their self-affirmation. We need the illusion of possessing a woman if we are to prove our uniqueness and our superiority over other men. And yet secretly we subject women to our scorn in order to conceal the way we misuse them and to be able to gloat about it among ourselves. This contempt often cements our relationship with other men. Together, we can think of women as inferior; yet above all we want to be accepted by them—accepted as flawless heroes.

Under these conditions, how can there be true intimacy, which presupposes equality? How can we attain it if *every moment we are together* we feel inadequate, superior, and/or guilty to the core of our being? *Inadequate* because deep inside we do not even believe in the myth of masculinity we have adopted; *superior* because we try to deceive ourselves with our myth; and *guilty* because our actual contempt for women belies our dependence on their recognition and admiration (a discrepancy then covered over by our arrogance).

The whole misfortune of the male compulsion to triumph over women is made clear in fantasies men have during the sex act. These fantasies are often completely impersonal and aggressive and reduce the woman to a random passive object. Why is it that many men can enjoy sex only with a woman who sells herself or who enables them to fantasize that she is a whore? By despising women, men can evade the genuine intimacy they fear because of doubts of their adequacy; they do not really believe that anyone could accept them unquestioningly. It seems to me that the reason we men need aggressive sexual fantasies is in order to compensate for our feelings of inadequacy.

Men are burdened with a compulsive need to perform well. This brings with it an insatiable need for praise and approbation, which in turn engenders an always present fear of botching the next performance. In *The Way of All Flesh* (1950), Samuel Butler, the nineteenth-century English novelist and satirist, addresses this plight, attempting to redress it when he has Edward's father say: "... We must judge men not so much by what they do, as by what they make us feel that they have it in them to do. ... It is not by what a man has actually put down upon his canvas, nor yet by the acts which he has set down, so to speak, upon the canvas of his life that I will judge him, but by what he makes me feel that he felt and aimed at" (p. 8). In his essay commemorating the one-hundredth anniversary of Goethe's death, included in *The Dehumanization of Art* (1956), Ortega y Gasset approaches the same problem somewhat differently: "Life is, in itself and forever, shipwreck. To be ship-wrecked is not to drown. ... Consciousness of shipwreck, being the truth of life, constitutes salvation. Hence I no longer believe in any ideas except the ideas of shipwrecked men" (pp. 126–27).

Unfortunately, what counts in our conventional system of values and norms is not our feeling side but solely what we attain in a "successful" career. That is how our worth is assessed by others; it is also the standard by which we judge ourselves. The yardstick by which a man is measured is success—not his ability to laugh, to play, or to be affectionate. But in the last analysis such success depends on someone else's failure. This lesson is first taught us by our parents and is then reinforced in school, so that by the time we reach adulthood, we are haunted by an internalized nightmare: in order to goad ourselves to be successful in our culture, we must learn to have nightmares about being a failure. Sociologist Jules Henry documents this situation with painful acuity in his book *Culture Against Man* (1963).

This pattern applies equally to men and women but with one major difference. In our culture most men have little chance of shaping their lives in a way that will free them from the metaphysics of achievement and success. And since these abstractions seemingly help us to attain a sense of adequacy, we accept them as essential needs. For women, on the other hand, another possibility enters into their development. Because they know from an early age that they are *potential bearers of life*, the *real* goal of bringing forth a life— and with it the possibility of enjoying it openly, of sharing in its pain and suffering, pleasure and happiness—can become the focal point of their self-concept. The sense of being that develops here does not depend on abstractions, but on aspirations and ultimately the real- ities of felt experience.

Since we men are not blessed with a comparable capacity to give birth, most of us build up a life-orientation that cuts us off from the joy and from the anticipation of pain and elation associated with bringing forth life.

Generally, this orientation also prevents us from acknowledging our fears. It is acceptable for a woman to devote herself to her child's fears and despair; for us, however, domination becomes the means by which we repress our fear. The result is that we develop a fear of fear itself, which keeps us from ever discovering that these fears will abate only when they can be accepted as such. Instead, we keep dreading them as ominous defeats. If we could understand this, we would discover that though our fear is of complete helplessness—it is actually of a helplessness pertaining to a specific situation. It does not have to be equated with total impotence and failure. Feeling helpless can instead lead to a recognition of the limits of one's influence and the ability to accept interdependency.

We are prevented from finding this out because it has always been impressed upon us that we must denounce all helplessness as weakness. We learn to regard every manifestation of helplessness around us as a threat that could lead to making *us* weak. With this, we became unable to accept others as our equals. The words of Cato, who was held up to us in school as the model of a moral and dutiful citizen of ancient Rome, illustrates the absurdity of male dominance, which only intensifies anxiety and makes impossible genuine relationships between men and women, as well as between men. In the second century before Christ, Cato called upon all men to oppress women, for as soon as they are given equal opportunity, he cautioned, they prove themselves to be superior (Fester et al. 1979, p. 8).

The price that must be paid for that kind of violence is a constant, nagging suspicion that, deep inside, one is living a lie. This is the fiction of superiority, which undermines all our relationships, whether with children, women, animals, nature, or ourselves. Both men and women live under the spell of this fiction, and since it arouses hatred in both, they become destructive toward each other. The man becomes irritable, angry, and ill-tempered because he has recurring anxiety dreams about coming defeat; the woman does injury to the man and to herself by holding him to his claim to be a hero.

Mutual contempt seethes secretly beneath the surface, for every man and every woman knows in his or her heart that there is not a man living who does not feel something of the helplessness that belies the myth he lives by. Perhaps this is the reason why there are so many who feel comfortable living with their mutual contempt, which corresponds to their own genuine feelings toward themselves.

What is actually at issue with us men? How conscious and authentic are we? Do we feel whole only if we are in charge, in possession? When we provide for and pay for someone else, we feel confident that we are loved, and at the same time we feel entitled to control that person. By affirming our position of power, our partner also exposes our deep feelings of inferiority, for we are being loved for proving ourselves, for the care we are providing—not for what we are as human beings. It is difficult for us to believe that we could be loved for ourselves, for our own emotions, for our joy and delight, our love of life. And so we slip ever deeper into the trap of having to prove ourselves. To be taken care of becomes a tacit agreement between the provider and the one provided for, to which both submit and whose price is a secret resentment and animosity. But the mechanism of the trap prevents us from calling a spade a spade. This would give the whole thing away: the necessity of resentment and the counterpower of reproach.

Thus it comes about that the partners in this kind of relationship express their suppressed resentment by increasing their demands on each other. The woman who submits to the man because he is providing for her keeps raising the stakes. This is her secret power. And the secret contempt on the part of the man who does the providing grows. After all, he thinks he has his partner in the palm of his hand. The trick lies in knowing how to play the game without endangering the whole arrangement. If one's maneuverings fail to bring what one wants, rage is the result. Since rage can't be expressed directly, because this would reveal that each is in the other's power and would ruin the surreptitious game of illusory love, psychosomatic symptoms then appear: for example, unacknowledged rage turns into a headache or a migraine. This is one of the reasons why psychosomatic disturbances are on the increase in our society.

It is here, in the form of headaches and migraine, that the deep-seated malaise stemming from the masculine ideas of superiority and need to dominate can be seen at its worst. *A self based on these ideas simply doesn't function; and since one is not allowed to admit it, a man has no choice but to bring ruin on himself and his world.* He fears that if he does not act as he does, everything will fall apart. And he is right insofar as there is indeed the danger that his personality will disintegrate if it is grounded primarily on power. He fears that the pact will be broken, the emotional game involving "who is providing for whom" ended, and the resulting self-degradation of both partners exposed. That poses a threat not only to family relationships but to *all* relationships that are based on power because the foundation for such a self-esteem has been undermined. In that case, there is danger of collapse, chaos, and great anxiety, for self-esteem that rests on power is not strong enough to sustain itself under challenge to its power ideology. The source of the hypocrisy that is destroying us is thus to be found in the way our self has developed.

We are afraid to start over, afraid to change, because we do not believe anyone could love us for being ourselves. And so we go on playing our self-destructive games, believing that the best teachers are those—psychotherapists included—who show us how to play the game better. Yet, if we—psychotherapists included—could be open, sincere, and authentic, we would not need to have headaches, for instance.

Our true self, that which we might have become, is concealed by the scenario of power. We were forced into its mold because no one liked us as we were. Small children, in their first and sometimes second year of life, show by their nonverbalized despair that they still perceive the truth. I say "nonverbalized" because their parents do not recognize this despair for what it is; they see it as ill humor and defiance. The feelings they were forced to deaden in themselves long ago they now reject as resistance in their children. Here we have a typical example of a very generalized form of projection in our society: the projection of hostility and aggressiveness onto our children.

The great misfortune is that, disregarding what our heart tells us, we live according to the ideolggy of a mutilated self, going along with preprogrammed kinds of love that are not love at all. In addition, there are people who play, as it were, a game within the game of "being loving." They are the truly evil ones. They hide their actions behind the lie of being loving and in so doing manage to get by. Since we are often in complicity with their game, we usually cannot afford to see through the situation. This explains the success of psychopaths in our society; to recognize them for what they are would force us to confront their false love, a mere parody of the real thing. Instead, we direct our anger at those who are seriously attempting to help us face reality.

The Oedipus Complex as Expression of the Male Myth of Power

Our betrayal of what we might have been, which lays the foundation for our destructive tendencies in general, is determined by our relationship with our mother. To say this is not to blame her, for in this regard she serves only as a link to the father and to society, where the self is predicated upon power as the sole worthwhile reality. It is this "reality" that creates the mother's need to exploit her child's dependency. When women are oppressed, they try to compensate for their disappointment and lack of self-fulfillment by means of their relationship with their children, especially if they themselves accept the ideology of male domination.[1] They may then in their turn seek power over and through their child, but they go about it in ways that mask their intent to dominate. A mother will "love" her children because she can use them as the instruments of her own will to power. What comes of this is then extolled—and concealed—by the Oedipal "myth": extolled because the child's feelings of despair are celebrated as love; concealed because what is involved here is in fact power and not love.

It is neither love nor sexuality in a strict sense that makes a little boy in the Oedipal stage want to possess his mother. Rather, this is brought about by her often unconscious rejection of his authentic self. The mother's desire to use her child as a tool for her power needs motivates him to cling to her, to placate her, to serve her—or to dominate her.

The grievous injury done to the mother in our society lies not only in her oppression but also in the fact of her adaptation to the myth of male superiority and her belief in her own worthlessness. To the extent that today's women's movement interprets equality as the right to be just as bad as the worst of men, it merely perpetuates men's domination in new ways. What is more, by denying the strength of the creative aspects of their love, women who subscribe to this interpretation continue to rear their children of both sexes to become adults who will in turn reject their authentic strength and opt for a ruthless pursuit of power. That is the real significance of the Oedipus complex: it has to do with a basic injury which metamorphoses into a striving for dominance.

People who are described as "neurotic" are simply still relatively modest in their hunger for power. They either fear it or consider it wrong. What is often termed "working through" an Oedipus complex in psychotherapy or psychoanalysis is actually a "liberation" from scruples and an encouragement of ambition, competitiveness, and greed for power. The deep wounds that once caused feelings of unacceptable helplessness and anxiety cannot really be reached in the kind of therapy that is hostage to the ideology of domination. But patients must confront these old wounds if they are to regain their lost humanity, which they have come to fear. This will not be possible, however, as long as therapists, for the sake of the male myth, remain unaware of their own feelings of powerlessness; they will be unable to help patients find the way back to their authentic self.

The Fear of Vitality

The "Oedipal" situation has further ramifications. As an expression of possession rather than of love, it gives rise to a fundamental deception. Again, it is the male conception of possession as power that comes into play. If possessing is equated with love, then the woman is thereby given the "power" to bestow the "love" on the man. A surprising twist perhaps! But what is the man actually attributing to the woman in his glorification of her? Isn't it the vitality and creative life-force *he* fends off within itself because he fears them? Men think about themselves in a logical, orderly way without realizing that it crushes their spontaneity, which they have grown to fear. Life is not logical and orderly: whatever is full of life is chaotic. This is disturbing to those men in particular who equate chaos with helplessness. Therefore, we invented the fiction of penis envy in order to escape having to notice that we want something specific from women—namely, that they grant us mastery over their vagina, which seems to us to be so alive, so full of vitality. Penis envy is a self-serving invention; it camouflages *our* envy of something that has eluded us and that we believe women possess: vitality and creativity. That is why we feel we must possess women, to whom we *attribute* these forces because we cannot ackowledge them in ourselves.

Of course there are women who have betrayed what they might have been by accepting male propaganda about masculine superiority. Such women seem to think they need the same kind of power that men claim for themselves alone, and they are prepared to do whatever is necessary to gain possession of that "magical strength" by means of their sexuality. Only here, in this context, does penis envy have any meaning. But from the moment these women actually gain possession of a man, they look upon him as inferior. Along with men's alleged superiority, they also appropriate men's contempt for women and must therefore despise themselves. Consequently, their lack of self-respect contaminates everything they possess.

In this sense, there *are* women with penis envy. They long for what only we men are supposed to possess: power. Freud turned this phenomenon into a driving life-force, confusing the phenotype with the genotype. In so doing, he characterized women as having a drive constellation that is actually merely a manifestation of the male mythology. At the same time, he obscured another situation: men are much more likely to place undue value on their penis, the more the creative side of life escapes them.

On the other hand, history has certainly produced men who have an intimate knowledge of life, of its beauty and splendors, be it a sunrise, a waterfall, or the gurgling of a baby. And there are societies, such as the African Ituri (Turnbull 1962) or the Yequana in the Venezuelan jungle, where men are whole human beings.[2] But in our society they are not.

It all begins with fear, the fear of being helpless, a fear so great that we block out all memory of the helplessness which characterizes the beginning of our human existence, instead of accepting it and integrating it into our experience. For many men, their rejection of this fundamental human quality reduces their life to a farce.

Why do men hate their helplessness so much? And why do many women, often those who are admired for being especially attractive and successful, hate helpless men? Helplessness is feared because it often has been the precondition for our subjugation. If parents take advantage of their children's helplessness by turning them into objects by means of which they preserve their own "self-esteem," these children will come to regard helplessness as the enemy. Therefore, it is not helplessness per se but its instrumental character, the way it is used by others in the context of our own experience of it, that makes it so threatening and unacceptable.

If children are never given cause to feel that they are loved and respected for their own sake, the helplessness with which they are confronted at every stage of their development elicits uncontrollable fear. Children's tiny size, their powerlessness, their insignificance—except as objects that make others feel significant—in short, their inferiority, make it impossible for them to discover their own self. Under such circumstances, children cannot gain a firm hold on themselves, for they are faced with a chaotic flood of sensory perceptions—an unbearable kind of helplessness.

They will then either experience psychic disintegration or find coherence in the structure provided by their parents. That is why helplessness is equated with the loss of the self. The classic way out of their despair over this is the one offered by society: power—specifically, power over others. Children sense the mutual exploitation in their parents' behavior. They empathize with their parents' secret despair and see through the apparent victories that come from the way their parents humiliate and disparage each other. Power—this the unspoken promise—is the cure for the child's situation.

Children know exactly when their parents are taking advantage of their helplessness and protracting it in order to prop up their own feelings of self-worth. And by repressing their spontaneous reactions, which are too threatening, children are able to live "in harmony" with their parents. They begin to believe that the world of their parents and the way their parents treat them are what is best for them. They then deny their own suffering and gradually forget how to listen to their inner voice. But the rage that is aroused because their autonomy has been destroyed becomes a destructive drive in its own right and stimulates their desire for power. If nothing happens to relieve their situation—if they are not treated humanely, for example—children soon learn that pain itself is an effective means of gaining power over others. They understand that pain can alter their own mood, and they begin to assume that everyone and everything can be controlled by inflicting it. It is to childish fantasies dealing with this subject that we should turn if we want to find the original motives behind the behavior of the grown men who wield power; in these fantasies we find too the first germs of the themes of our "history."

Men Are More Impaired than Women

The origins of yet another situation are also to be found here. Given the conditions of a culture that advocates power as the guiding principle for the self, many children learn to pretend they have been hurt in order to manipulate those who actually have injured them. They are quick to learn the hypocrisy that permeates the world of power: the expression of psychic pain in the form of depression and various types of withdrawal irritates adults; whereas a deceptive maneuver, such as eyes filled with tears, is more likely to arouse sympathy and give adults a sense of power. The obvious success of this manipulative game should not blind us to the source of great contempt it represents! This is how deceitfulness is perpetuated. To manipulate the world with lies means to betray the self.

With such circumstances as these playing a role in our development, it is difficult for both men and women to accept their helplessness as a precondition for being able to listen to what the self is saying; yet even greater pressure is placed on men to submit to the ideology of power, with the result that the concept of the self that emerges destroys their humanity. As already mentioned, women often have a greater possibility of finding a meaning to existence outside the confines of this ideology because they are able to bring life into the world. Probably many men have been saved because of their relationship to a mother for who reality meant concrete experience and not a metaphysical system—experience, for instance, of the helplessness of her children whose aliveness is for her a source of pleasure. This is not, however, to laud the drudgery and the excessive ties to home and household that so often go hand in hand with maternal child rearing in our culture.

The decisive point is that many women, in spite of their situation, have been willing to be receptive to their children's helplessness; they have integrated it with their own vitality and the pleasure they take in their children and do not experience it as threatening or burdensome; and, for this reason, neither do their children. The mother guides her children toward the discovery that they are being encouraged to reach out for and grasp the world. Such receptivity on the mother's part, made possible by an awareness of her own creative powers, also strengthens her ability to empathize. Her maternal empathy furthers the child's growth through her dependable and appropriate response to his or her needs and at the same time reinforces the mother's own feelings of adequacy, strength, and happiness.

Actually, we could all be sensitive to the helplessness of a being whom we protect and nurture and whose development we are involved in. But if the way our self is structured discourages such an attitude as a sign of weakness and inadequacy, then the opportunity will be missed. Since our culture places greater pressure on men than on women to produce a self that finds helplessness offensive, a fundamental difference arises in the way this state is dealt with.

We must come to terms with the fact that the difference furthers *primarily* in women greater realism and open-mindedness to reality. They are more humane than men in the sense that they are less cut off from their feelings, less inclined to try to escape them by way of abstractions.

As I have indicated, every age has brought forth men who have known how to respond to the helplessness of others in a protective way, who have neither feared it nor felt devastated by it. But in our culture, dominated by the veneration of power, it is women, with their greater openness to reality, who, far more than men, must live on two levels. This is because their most profound experiences contradict official reality. In other words, if official logic and the feelings that derive from personal experience are not isomorphic (do not coincide), integration of the two levels is not possible.

We men frequently take this as an indication that women are to varying degrees "hysterical," prone to irrationality, and illogical. What a simplistic and strange self-deception on our part! But a contemptuous attitude toward women helps men to retain their deluded assumptions about the supposed necessity to be "strong" and powerful.

How can women be expected to have anything but a divided self when the "rationality" of power contradicts their openness and flexibility, their creative potential, vitality, and tenderness, as well as their acceptance of helplessness and suffering? If they do not submit to the dictates of logic, they are quickly accused of being inconsistent. Men's "logic" rejects women's "inconsistent" responses while regarding male behavior as consistent.

I believe we should be grateful that mutability and irrationality still exist, for they are what keep us in touch with life. We would all be more like robots than we already are if every mother allowed herself to be pressured into cutting off her feelings. The fact that there is any psychic health left in our world speaks for the strength and pervasiveness of the ability to have direct experiences that are rooted in genuine needs and goals.

We men must try to make clear to ourselves how detrimental are the barriers separating us from those needs which stem from helplessness, psychic pain, and the bringing forth of new life. These same barriers have increased our separation from the reality of being alive, from ourselves, from women and children.

In the past, if women wanted to retain their ties to real feelings, they had to devote a part of their life to showing admiration for their ambitious husbands and acclaim for designated heroes. This was what permitted them to create a space in which their other self could express itself without too much outside interference. Children and home (without glorifying attendant drudgery) provided the opportunity for women to develop a kind of freedom and psychic health for themselves under the cloak of female "inferiority."

When I see women who believe attainment of equal rights means the freedom to be as ambitious and power hungry as the most "manly" of men,[3] I fear that they will have a harmful effect on those members of their own sex who have managed to remain whole in their own way. For the latter will have to defend themselves not only against men but also against those women who have accepted the masculine view of freedom. The "freedom" to pursue power in order to avoid having to face one's fears burdens women with the same contempt men feel for the female sex. A self that turns its back on helplessness is able to experience portions of its inner life only to a very limited extent. It cannot deal with its own fears and uncertainties but instead attempts to negate them by feeling contempt for others and by trying to become invulnerable. This is of course a vain struggle for both men and women; helplessness, for the very reason that it is feared, lurks around every corner. The desperate chase only leads to paranoia, defensiveness, saber rattling, and the insanity of the arms race.

Admiration

Dependence on admiration—that is, on being admired—seems to promise to bring the "strength" we long for. Men want to be admired for "being strong." The admiration they are given is called love; whereas it is actually more than likely to stifle real love. Usually, this is not the conscious intent, but it turns out that way in practice.

If we want to be loved for conquests and heroic deeds that are based on fear, on the fear that in reality we might be weak, we will despise ourselves as well as those who "love" us for these achievements. Accordingly, we want to be admired all the more, for then we need not pay attention to our doubts and will feel loved. But the real love we all desire will elude us, as will intimacy, that closeness we need but at the same time fear, since it requires openness and authenticity. Caught up in the untruths of an abstract "masculinity," many men never succeed in finding their self in intimate relationships. Thus, a nonself is perpetuated. How can a man (or woman) be admired for something that is ulti-mately predicated on self-deception? As long as the fear of being helpless, a fear that must be concealed even from oneself, is the cause of this deception, those who do the admiring must deny their own helplessness and so lose themselves. Calculation and manipulation—in other words, duplicity—may be all that re-mains. No matter how successful someone may be on this level, it has nothing to do with love!

A patient of mine helped me gain an understanding of this type of admiration. During one of our sessions, she cried out: "My last resort was to become a part of my mother, to be just like her. What a trick I was playing! When I admired her for the way she was, she couldn't find me! I wasn't there any more!" A remarkable insight: if we become like the powerful person we idealize, then no one can find us. We aren't there! The price we all must pay in this game is the loss of self and, consequently, the loss of closeness to the other person.

There is another, highly ambivalent aspect of admiration. The one who does the admiring can exercise power, a power given by the one who wants to be admired! A paradox—but true, nevertheless! We use admiration and idealization to bring down those we idealize. This is the revenge of the oppressed: "You aren't the way you promised to be!" The person we have believed in can from one moment to the next be overthrown and destroyed. Since history is full of such reversals, why have we always been so credulous? Is it because people do not have sufficient intelligence or education? I believe that is a misleading explanation, which only shields us from the truth: namely, that we submit to our oppressors in order to lose our self but secretly hold them fast to their alleged godlikeness, so that we can be sure of avenging ourselves one day. In the case of tyrants and dictators we do not admit our true motivation—unless they are already falling from power—but in our relationships with our less threatening fellow humans it can be seen at work every day. We idealize our husband or wife or some other "love" object, which means we never need to get close to the real person but only to the one we have imagined. Then one day our admiration is gone; the other person had disappointed us. This is the trick we use in order never to lose ourselves in the kind of close attachment we all experienced long ago in childhood. In those days we still dared to be open to our helplessness, but we were often taken advantage of as a result; that is the source of the pain and the trauma that make us try to escape our real need for love and closeness. If we were conscious of this connection, we would have to confront the self that is based on power. Instead, we idealize, we tell ourselves that we are full of admiration and love, and we hold each other at arm's length.

To the extent that we make others admire us, we also give them power over us. Consequently, men play games with women and women with men, each becoming the self-appointed arbiter of the other's strength. Both have power, although both feel incapable of living their own life. What we are presented with here is the sight of men pursuing women and women pursuing men, all in search of a hallucinatory power residing in their counterpart, with each one hating the other because they both feel they are under the other's sway.

Oedipus Once Again

Where does the myth of male superiority lead us? Essentially, it is not love we are seeking but the woman or man who will strengthen us. We soon become entangled in a web of hatred, even though we believe our pursuit of an extraordinary partner is a search for love. This drives the man on, not only to ever greater achievements, but also to heart attacks, depression, or suicide. For the woman this often results in her becoming that sort of ambitious mother who calls it love when she uses her children as tools of her own self-assertion. In the end, possessiveness serves as the only valid reality in human relationships for everyone— men, women, and children. To possess someone is power and bestows power. We usually aren't aware of this if things are going well, except when we think back to all the times we felt *threatened* in our claim to possess a man, woman, friend, or child. Who has not felt the danger signals deep inside if our wife speaks with enthusiasm about another man—or even about another woman? Or if our child praises someone else's father (or mother)?

Thus, many men are prone to feel abandoned, offended, under attack, wounded. This begins at an early age, and the feelings of imminent abandonment and of betrayal are referred to as the Oedipus complex, which is a kind of boomerang in that it expresses men's need for superiority and dominance. This built-in vengefulness results from a dehumanizing process in which power is exchanged for love. The Oedipus complex, that sweeping theory about the love sons have for an unattainable mother, simply ignores the ramifications the father's domination of the mother has for her and thus for the child.

If little boys feel that they cannot separate from their mother, perhaps this is caused by the way some women succeed in making their sons overly attached to them. Direct seductiveness produces the same result as unattainability: in both cases, the child learns that what matters most is to possess the other person.

With extraordinary perceptiveness, the Nobel Prize-winning dramatist Eugene O'Neill struggled with the problems of attachment and its ramifications in all his works, most particularly in *More Stately Mansions* (1964). In this play, a mother, overpowered by a male dominated world that prevents her from finding self-realization, seeks refuge in romantic fantasies which transport her out of her misery—but are themselves based upon the allure of the male pursuit of power! For her son, this daily withdrawal into a fantasy world spells abandonment. In a family in which possession of the other person is equated with "love," the son can only conclude that he is not loved, since his mother distances herself from him, that is, is not interested in possessing him. He therefore tries all his life to gain access to her "dream house." (The mother in the drama always flees to the summerhouse, where she can dream her fantasies undisturbed.) Her son hopes that if he can only gain entry to this house, he will become the object of her possessiveness and will thereby win the "love" she has been withholding. What he finally comes to realize one day as an adult is the emptiness of her efforts to possess anyone and the fact of her rage and her madness. At the same time, he becomes aware of these same tendencies in himself and goes mad.

The drama that unfolds here is not about love but about possessiveness. Since we call the latter love, it arouses feelings in us that make us capable of killing and/or dying for it. If a mother gives her son the illusory impression that he can possess her (or, in O'Neill, that he can *not* possess her), she is playing him off against his father. The father—or his proxy in the mother's psyche—therefore becomes the son's rival. This pitting of son against father (and vice versa) has its origin in the entangling power struggles that take place between men and women. A boy will have the feeling that he is losing his mother to his father only if he has the need to possess her, a need she originally awakens in him because she is unable to find fulfillment in genuine self-realization as a result of being dominated by her husband.

The anger that men's domination engenders in women usually remains hidden from those it involves. But when everything in a relationship revolves around possession, how should women be expected to react if not by making a game of letting themselves be possessed and using this as a weapon? It presents no problem to bring a son to the point of rivalry with his father if the boy feels he has never adequately possessed his mother: the mother simply doesn't give him the attention and love he needs, or she puts him off with promises of what he might be given if only he finds the magic key. The Freudian interpretation of the Oedipus myth obscures the fact that possessiveness is a stratagem in the destructive game in which men dominate women and which is not an expression of love but its distortion.

"Superiority"

Men are deeply tormented by doubts about their superiority. Although their doubts are usually concealed, now and then a man who himself has been loudest in proclaiming his masculine superiority will disavow it. I knew one such man whose self-assurance depended to a great degree upon his exercise of power and who had an image that was highly regarded. He was continually chasing beautiful women and usually meeting with success, even though his behavior toward them was "mean and vile" (his own words). He once confided to me, "If you humiliate someone enough, you don't have to worry, because then you have that person on *your* level." There you have the truth about this kind of male self-assurance!

Men want love, but they are caught in a vicious cycle because their "superiority" makes them turn women into mothers who are unable to give their sons real love. This is bad enough in itself, but since women's compliance makes them hide their hostility toward the male sex both from themselves and the rest of the world, their sons find themselves in a highly confusing plight: the mother acts as though she accepts her son but in reality rejects him. I have described this situation in a research article entitled "Maternal Rejection and Children's Intensity" (1980b): it seems that men's relationship with their mother is much more ambiguous than is the case for women who also have experienced maternal rejection.

It is interesting that in his study of male psychological health, the psychiatrist G. E. Vaillant (1978) found a preponderant tendency to develop in a schizoid and overideational way in those men who were dominated by their mother into adulthood. This is exactly what happens when a boy has a mother who is full of contradictions he cannot fathom. Thus, the victims of male superiority are not only women but their sons as well.

Unfortunately, this situation is not easy to detect, since countless men run after those very women who basically have nothing to give them. The pathology I am referring to here is the great quest for love in those quarters where none is to be found. The woman who has nothing to offer becomes the object of our intense desire. The tacit assumption is that *women who don't show love must be hiding it, withholding it; women who want to give love, on the other hand, can't be worth anything—if they were, they would hide it as their most treasured possession!*

Salvation and "Sanctity"

The male myth destroys men and everything they touch. Of course, it does not influence us all to the same degree. But it is always there at hand because we need it if we are to avoid confronting our own self, which fills us with fear. How else can we explain the fact that again and again we submit to those very people who, personifying the epitome of strength and domination, demand the greatest self-sacrifice of us? Nothing evokes a messianic atmosphere—a feeling of sanctity—more than subordination to a "higher" cause. The call to shed one's blood for God, for nation, or for an idea elicits feelings of inner purity, the exhilaration of absolute "love," the intoxication of virtuous self-love. Why is it that we never recognize until later, when the episode has gone down in history, that here was a case of subjection to a powerful madman? Often the best among us are involved, those who want to be free, who forsake everything dear to them. They turn against their own principles and their own feelings when a dictator, *Führer*, "spiritual leader," prime minister, or *duce* summons them to battle—and they feel ennobled. What does this virtuous feeling of sanctity have to do with the true self? Why do we men—and many women—repeatedly behave like sheep, especially when confronted with those who most despise, dominate, oppress, and destroy us? Why does obeying them make us feel so good? Why does it release us from the anxiety and uneasiness of having a self of our own, from having to take responsibility for ourselves?

Is fear of our helplessness so deeply imprinted in us men that we run into the arms of every leader who offers us salvation through shelter in his *contempt for us?* Yes, his contempt for us and for our life saves us because we despise ourselves. Our struggle to conquer, to attain power, superiority, and success conceals our ever-present fear of failure and helplessness, which we have learned to regard only as weakness. In spite of the most astonishing achievements, we still doubt our "masculinity." If our partner doesn't have an orgasm, for example, we immediately take this as a reflection of our lack of virility!

The oppressor frees us from our secret self-contempt by his contempt for us. How else does a Stalin become a father figure, a Hitler a flawless god? *We* glorify them—and then feel ennobled ourselves—because deep down we recognize *their* inferiority, emptiness, and hatred of life. To the present day, historians attribute magical gifts to Hitler in order to explain how the whole world could have succumbed to him. But the reasons lie primarily in ourselves: we ascribe to such leaders qualities they do not possess because their contempt sets us free.

Richard Nixon provides an illustration from recent history. When he was running on the Republican ticket with Eisenhower in 1952, everyone knew that he was guilty of accepting illegal funds. (As a senator he had received $18,235 from several California businessmen and used the money for personal purposes [White 1975]). He actually confessed to this when he defended himself on television[4] in a speech in which he pleaded for his viewers' compassion. Yet people felt comfortable with him and not with Adlai Stevenson, who was an honorable man.

Kurt Tucholsky's description of one of Hitler's speeches is apt here: "Something strange ... then came nothing at all ... nothing, nothing, nothing. No suspense, no high points, he wasn't gripping; after all, I am too much the artist not to admire artistry if it were there, even in the likes of him. No humor, no warmth, no fire, nothing. Nor does he say anything but the most stupid banalities, draws conclusions that aren't conclusions at all—nothing" (Schuls 1959, p. 156).

That must be the way it is: we endow such figures with the life we fear for the very reason that they project the hatred we accept as an ersatz for life and free us from the obligation to lead a real and responsible life. *We* are our own enemy; *they* could not destroy our souls if we were not willing partners. It is not enough to fight against these psychopathic murderers; we must also discover what our own needs are that make us keep our inner emptiness at bay. Consider two such different "statesmen" as Chamberlain and Stalin, who were both taken in by Hitler. Under the cover of "sanctity" lent by our submissiveness, are we not expressing our own ruination through destroying others, the "enemies" against whom we take revenge for our unacknowledged wounds?

It is our children, who we do not allow to have a self, who take revenge on us and on the world by sacrificing themselves to their last breath for a leader, holy man, or god. History is full of examples of the "heroic deeds" of children in wars and battles; even today they run through mine fields and die for "higher causes" *because they do not have a self.* Whether we are speaking of the Children's Crusade, the youth organizations of totalitarian states, or children who betray their parents by reporting them to the authorities, a widespread phenomenon under Hitler and Stalin, don't we see a travesty of the true self in their submission to an ideology? Submission is supposed to lead to the self! One of life's paradoxes, a horrendous situation in which dissolution of the self becomes one's goal in life! Over and over again the oppressors are well served, for underneath the "idealism" and "noble motives" of their victims lurks the stored-up rage of the wounded child whose autonomy has been impaired.

This does not apply to everyone, not to Hermann Hesse in *Demian*, for instance, or to other artistic souls who have repeatedly showed us other paths to take. Some, perhaps many, find the way back to themselves in spite of social pressure. Fear enables some to be strong within themselves instead of complying with an ideology of strength. In a moving illustration of this, Sophie and Hans Scholl, a sister and brother who were students at the University of Munich, and their circle of friends, out of deep moral conviction resisted Hitler during the terrible years of 1942 and 1943 (Ilse Scholl 1977).

Caroline Muhr states it differently in her novel *Freundinnen* (Women Friends) (1974): ". . . Old men always look much more lonely than old women, much more helpless." She means that men have more to lose—and lose it more quickly—than women: power (and the self-assurance it brings), the very thing that men pursue, keeps slipping through their fingers. Women, on the other hand, are more content, for "they have been used to losing for a long time."

There is much in our life that is false to the core. A man fights for a self that is not a true self. It is only a shell, dependent on abstractions that do not serve life itself but rather its conceal-ment. Women who are true to themselves—that is, who are in touch with their own authentic life-forces—are never in favor of war. Men for whom the same applies are also against war. Fre-quently, however, those who resist the ideology of power are persecuted, for their existence is a threat to the perpetuation of the lie. It has been ever thus.

We can take the Gnostics as an illustration. Nearly two thou-sand years ago they were viewed as heretics by Christianity, which was gradually becoming institutionalized and needed an ideology of power and oppression in order to become dominant. While the church bureaucracy was establishing its role according to the model provided by Rome—unconditional belief in author-ity, in one Catholic church, in one truth, and therefore one bishop, like Caesar—Gnostics were writing about the way humanity was being undermined by power.

Tertullian (ca. A.D. 190), for example, was upset by the fact that the Gnostics did not make hierarchical distinctions among priests, bishops, and the faithful. In her book *The Gnostic Gospels* (1979), Elaine Pagels documents his horror that women were given equal rights with men. It is interesting that the church, although opposed to Rome, identified with Rome as the paragon of power. For both the Church and Rome, the soul rested on an ideology of power. (Regarding this, Mario Erdheim brings us into the present with his essay, "Nach aller Regel" [Following the Rules] [1981]. He focuses on the phenomenon of unconscious identification with power: "What Horkheimer and Adorno called 'the dialectic of the Enlightenment' is also the product of unre- solved ambivalence on the part of the Enlightenment's adherents, who were aware that they were critical of power but not that they identified with it." It must be said, however, that what Erdheim calls ambivalence is a psychoanalytic oversimplification. The self is so firmly entrenched in the idea of dominating that it cannot free itself from this idea without disintegrating, unless—as is the case for women and some men—it is still rooted in an affirmative orientation toward life.)

In her book on the Gnostics, Pagels quotes a follower of Valentinius: "[These Christians] 'wanted to command one another, outrivalling one another in their empty ambition'; they are inflated with 'lust for power,' 'each one imagining that he is superior to the others' " (pp. 40–41).[5] The Gnostics, on the other hand, met as equals, loved one another, and helped one another in a spontaneous way. Women and men had equal rights. They understood that a person who joins a group can misuse it by exerting group pressure to gain control over someone else. They recognized the quest for power of those who out of self- contempt adhered submissively to a gourp norm for the sake of oppressing others: "You must think and act the same way I do, otherwise you are my enemy."

The implicit message ("See how I am sacrificing myself"), never said in so many words, lends a feeling of sanctity, even as one is committing the most dreadful deeds. One's own despised situa- tion and the misdeeds it engenders are thereby concealed. Actu- ally, this kind of destructiveness is brought about by self-hatred. In this context, martyrdom represents a love of death, not of life. When Ignatius, the bishop of Antioch, was condemned to torture and death by the Romans around A.D. 117, he admonished his fellow believers not to try to save him: "Let there come upon me fire, and the cross, and struggle with wild beasts, cutting and tearing apart, racking of bones, mangling of limbs, crushing of my whole body ... may I but attain to Jesus Christ!" (Pagels 1979, pp. 82–83). He wanted to be torn apart by wild animals to prove his faithful devotion to Christ.

Persecution and danger are sought out because they justify hatred toward others. And the *others* here were not the Romans but those who wanted to destroy the ideology of power, which was the underpinning—just as it was for the Romans—for a sense of self that was dependent on the need to dominate, on a feeling of superiority, on the oppression of others. Thus, in A.D. 177 in the French city of Lyon—where fifty Christians, including their bishop, had just been tortured to death—it was possible for Irenaeus to be free of hostility toward the Romans but full of hatred for the Gnostics, who regarded enthusiasm for martyrdom as a betrayal of life and of Christ and his teachings.

Again, we can recognize parallels here to modern times. We need only remember that Stalin did not hate Hitler but did hate Trotskyites and idealists—not those who were against him but those who jeopardized his personal self-deception.

The Gnostics knew that only an inner transformation leads to genuine well-being, something far different from the "salvation" that comes from being given approbation by an authority figure we have submitted to. The Gospel according to Saint Mark reports that the disciples thought of Jesus as their appointed King (Mark 8:27–29). The apocryphal *Gospel of Thomas* tells the story differently: "Jesus said to his disciples, 'Compare me to someone and tell me whom I am like.' Simon Peter said to him, 'You are like a righteous angel.' Matthew said to him, 'You are like a wise philosopher.' Thomas said to him, 'Master, my mouth is wholly incapable of saying whom you are like.' Jesus said, 'I am not your master. Because you have drunk, you have become drunk from the bubbling stream which I have measured out'" (Pagels 1979, p. 130).

In this version, Jesus is speaking of the deeper sense in which authority can be accepted without surrendering the self. In such a case, acknowledgment of authority can even result in psychological growth. The Gnostics, both women and men, knew in their own way what we today often forget: the socialization process can force us into dependency and infantilism. If we are unable to grow out of this, we will yearn to conform to some kind of authority. The *central lesson* life then teaches us is obedience; our behavior is considered desirable if it convinces authority figures of our willingness to be accommodating. The development of an amoral and unthinking attitude of mutual affirmation is the result, a patting each other on the back, a permanent smile that says, "You're OK, I'm OK," and assures our rise in a (career) group. These behavioral roles—packaged in images of kindness, fatherliness, motherliness, or respectfulness—hide the intention of the person on top to dominate and to exploit the dependence of the subordinate.

Siegfried Bernfeld, one of the early psychoanalysts, who was interested in casting light on the human condition, came to the conclusion that even in psychoanalysis, a discipline that is supposed to be concerned with liberating people, dependence on the good will of an authority figure is encouraged as a valuable "reality trait." His essay, "On Psychoanalytic Training" (1962), is a treatment of the contemporary institution of psychoanalysis, whose goal is to liberate but which treats its followers as objects of abstract rules. If this is the case, then how is it possible for autonomy, growth, and freedom to be encouraged in psychoanalysis—or, for that matter, in other movements which are initially revolutionary and dedicated to human renewal but which later become institutions? Institutions, whose structures are determined by the ideology of power, will certainly not provide such encouragement. As a consequence, institutionalization must always be resisted if the human dimension is to be preserved.

The terrible thing about the human condition is that when people are subjected to the lie of power and suffer from it, they nevertheless identify with power. They may exchange one *form* of it for another and consider themselves rebels, but everything they do represents a repetition of their self-surrender, not the creation of an authentic self.

The suffering involved in discovering one's own self is of an entirely different nature from the suffering that opts for salvation by identifying with something outside the self. Only those who can endure their own suffering are capable of establishing themselves as a *separate entity*. If we always hope, as Proust put it, that the person who caused our suffering is the same one who has the power to lessen our pain, then we will believe in the lie of power, always searching for the authority figure who will corroborate the lie and never finding what is divine in ourselves.

What determines this distinction in our suffering? It may be the way a child is treated by a mother whose love flows from her inner strength and lends the child strength to be true to his or her own feelings before being exposed to the world of the father. If, however, the mother—herself the prisoner of an oppressive husband—must make use of her child to prove her self-esteem (which is based on accommodating her husband), then her encounter with her child turns into a test of power. Under these conditions, a child's development of self will be stunted and remain at the level of an unstilled longing[6] and a waiting for gratification that never comes. Helplessness now becomes unbearable and something to be feared, and the child becomes a victim of the *central lesson* exemplified by the parents' relationship with each other and with the child: that power makes the person who exercises it less helpless. Even very young children perceive that their mother believes she feels stronger if she takes advantage of their helplessness.

Such experiences are rooted in preverbal and prelogical developmental stages. In a literal sense, we do not *know* anything of our early history. What we might have known is hidden by the distortions that serve to camouflage parental intentions. We then learn at an early age that if we want the relationship with our parents to be bearable, we must see them as they wish to be seen and not as they really are. In so doing, we lose sight of our own life and goals, placing our hopes in those who have promised to relieve our suffering. Strangely, Proust did not notice that a secret desire for revenge lies behind this attitude. "You *must* soothe my pain, otherwise you aren't worth anything"—this is the unspoken reproach to which we devote the rest of our life.

It is in the etiology of a self characterized by the oppression and domination of others—women in particular—that the source of human self-destructiveness and evil can be found. Many men sense how wrong their outlook is. Somewhere, sometime, perhaps only when they were very young, they had experiences of a contrary nature—deriving from their closeness to an empathic mother who accepted them so that through her and their own "searching mouth," as Erikson (1958) poetically expressed it, they were brought into contact with their mother's delight and love.

But the discrepancy between the two kinds of experience makes such men furious, for they are caught in a vicious circle of self-doubt. They cannot believe in their own truth and thus— neither well adapted nor revolutionary—are unable to relate to others. They are the truly lost ones. Their rage finds release in destructive outbursts, sometimes with fatal consequences. But they are not really evil; rather, they are desperate, especially when they are still in touch with their feelings. It is the others, those who pass off the mythology of the masculine lie as truth, against whom we must protect ourselves. In our confusion, it is they who can manipulate us, for they play with our helplessness until we are willing to accept the solution they have to offer. And the proferred salvation always promises, in the guise of noble goals, the collective discharge of the rage stored up inside us. War, conquest, national unity are all capable of rousing our energies and making us relinquish what remains of our self.

Freud was not entirely on the right track when he suggested sublimation as the antidote to rage and aggression. When arrogance leads one nation to go to war to crush another nation, when people persecute and destroy one another out of religious or ideological motives or devastate the environment in the name of progress—that is sublimation. Sublimation masks the destructive urge but does not alter it. If we are to eliminate or even reduce this disastrous urge, we must first discover the truth about the ideology of our self, for that is where the origin of our destructiveness lies.

It is essential for men to face their fear and helplessness, for that is the only way they can become conscious of their rage and its real origin. Only then can they focus their attention on those specific aspects of their life that produced their dilemma. Then they will be able to overcome their rage and to free themselves from their feelings of helplessness, as well as rage. By accepting helplessness, instead of defining it as weakness and inadequacy, they can come to see themselves as an integral part of a larger interconnected world.

A man who comes to accept his limitations in this way will be able to recognize forces outside himself without judging himself defective and will be able to relinquish his grandiosity. This releases him from his primitive and destructive rage, something that is not accomplished by repression or by sublimation; on the contrary, they both contribute toward keeping the source of his rage alive. Confronting our helplessness leads to the only strength that matters, the strength to face up to our weakness. Once we take this step, we discover that it does not destroy us to admit to our weaknesses and that it is now possible for us to gain genuine command of the self. All else is evasion. If we truly accept women as our equals, if we don't misuse them by making them into a means to avoid facing our self-doubts, we men will have gained the basic capacity for confronting our self.

IV

Without a Past We Cannot Laugh at Ourselves: The Significance of Stimulation for the State of Aliveness

IN general, every organism requires stimulation in order to stay and feel alive. Stimulation is necessary for the beginning of life itself and for its subsequent development; it is responsible for the organization of the organs and of their functions. Human beings are shaped to a large extent by the quality of the stimulus intensities affecting them. Roffwarg, Muzio, and Dement (1966) suggest that both in utero and right after birth, before there is sufficient external stimulation for the central nervous system, REM sleep (and attendant dreaming) serves as an endogenous source of stimulation. In their view, this contributes to the structural maturation and differentiation of key sensory and motor areas of the central nervous system and prepares them for the sudden influx of stimuli in postnatal life. The abrupt decrease in REM sleep that initiates with an infant's further development indicates that the maturing brain has less need of endogenic stimulation.

Stimulation remains a crucial factor, however. Research on sensory deprivation has shown that an uninterrupted stream of external stimuli is a prerequisite for the organization of metabolism, which in turn is an essential trigger for all activity, from care of the young to problem solving.[1] An infant who experiences no human warmth and affection, for instance, will die; the satisfaction of its purely physical needs is not sufficient.[2] An adult who is even partially deprived of stimulation (involving sight, sound, touch, smell) may develop mental disorders, frequently even insanity.[3]

We are surrounded to a great extent by a sea of stimuli: music, radio, television, advertising, pictures, street noises, newspapers, books, architecture, clothing, colors, et cetera—which we human beings have created ourselves. These stimuli have less to do with our purely physical survival needs than they do with our psychological state. Remove them from our environment and we will usually feel empty, bored, and apathetic. Indeed, we can say that we seek such stimuli unthinkingly in order to give ourselves the feeling of being alive. This means that we aren't free to choose on a conscious level those stimuli which reinforce that feeling. The lack of choice and our resultant dependency are hidden from us so long as we are unable to make our compulsions and dependency conscious. To be more precise I ought perhaps to say that there are people who are *not* dependent in the sense just described; they are able to choose without being conscious of having this ability. Between these two poles of being able or unable to choose one's stimuli there are many transitional and hybrid forms.

Our ability or inability to choose depends upon the quality of the stimulus world which we were exposed to in early life and which subsequently forces us more and more into different paths of development. This explains the fact that, although we all live in the same world in one sense, we seek out different types of stimuli, with the result that we ultimately exist in different worlds.

The types of stimulation we encounter can be divided into two basic categories: the first type touches our interior world and relates to our own feelings and needs; the second makes us into mere conveyors of preprogrammed reactions, like machines with their *input* and *output*. Since the stimuli in the first category affect our inner world, they always lead to a new inner integration. This in turn produces corresponding reactions, each of which expresses the self through a new creative act. Such reactions represent a continually new integration of outer and inner elements. The second type of stimulation, which cannot bring about any direct access to our interior world, is a sign of a diminished consciousness and cannot create anything in its turn but a diminished consciousness.

Both types of stimulation give people the motion they require for their sense of aliveness. (I am not speaking here of those whose life is an attempt to exclude motion and contact with the external world—in other words, those who fundamentally prefer death to "life.") Both basic categories of stimuli are life oriented, but they differ in their nature and in their implications for human existence.

An example: taken as a whole, urban architecture of the nineteenth century may be considered ugly. Yet if we let our gaze pass over a public building of the time, we will find that our eyes are satisfied. They will linger over this or that detail, will unconsciously fill out a line, a curve, an angle, and in the end we will feel a sense of gratification. Something has taken place; somehow we were induced to add something of our own, to contribute something to the act of perception. An active process was encouraged, one that brought our own creativity into play.

There is often a difference, however, when we let our eyes skim over the facade of the average modern building. It may be impressive, even give a sense of forcefulness; yet when we are finished, we will still find ourselves looking for something more. The eye is not "satisfied," yet we are not encouraged to participate in the act of perceiving. Although the observer perhaps even has been given a direct feeling of power through the experience, it is not truly satisfying, for it compels us simply to look for more stimulation.

This example demonstrates that our stimulus world is no longer able to touch or affect us in an interior sense. It forces us to search out more and more stimuli, which then will affect us only externally.

The spiraling effect will continue, and we will become what is called "stimulus-bound."

In order to be able to feel alive, we will need more and more external excitation, and to be stimulus-bound will become a consuming drive. The stimuli themselves will force us into an addictive mode, even though they leave us inwardly empty. Since we think that all we require is more of them in order to fill up the emptiness, our need will grow for what actually increases the void. There are numerous stimuli of this sort: loud music, large cars, glittering colors without nuances, gleaming machines—anything, so long as it delivers a higher degree of stimulation. What we will finally seek for our feeling of aliveness is simply the speed with which a change in stimuli takes place. The form or content of the stimulus itself will have scarcely any significance for us. In fact, empty forms will be preferred, since those with content and meaning slow down the tempo of change. To find meaning in an experience requires, after all, an act of mental organization and that takes time.

The consciousness shaped by our contemporary stimulus-world is a shrunken one. Formed by abstract concepts about our existence, this consciousness diminishes more and more severely those who are exposed to its effects. Proceeding increasingly from the assumption that people are machines with input and output features, it blocks their access to an inner life, preventing the development of their interior world; people will then end by corresponding exactly to the image of them posited in the first place. In psychology, this phenomenon is almost a consciously intended one. The American professor of psychology B. F. Skinner and his school—with their lasting influence on behavioral psychology throughout the world—treat human beings as if freedom and dignity were nonexistent. (*Beyond Freedom and Dignity* is the title of one of Skinner's most famous books!) The scientific accuracy of such premises is then "proved" by the fact that people actually become the way they are presumed to be. In this way, they become homogenized and simplified, and no connection is seen between their psychic malaise, induced by the inaccessibility of their interior world, and the preceding reduction of their potential human dimensions.

Another instance of our impairment as a result of a reductive emphasis on abstract concepts—this one less conscious or intentional—can be found in modern architecture. Hugo Kükelhaus (1978), a European writer on the philosophy of architecture, has pointed out that most of us never experience light as an unfolding living process. This way of experiencing light occurs, for example, in a forest as a matter of course but almost never under the conditions of contemporary architecture, which conceives light as something that must fall on or through extended unbroken surfaces (the larger the better). As a a result, light entering a structure can never be perceived as being in motion.

The decisive point is that the examples just discussed produce an impoverishment in the stimuli enlivening our interior world; and therefore we increasingly lose the ability to perceive the resonance of inner stimulation and are robbed of those experiences that enrich our sense of aliveness.

Relevant too in this context is the research of H. G. Birch, the late American psychologist, ethologist, and neurologist, who demonstrated many years ago (1950) that cats who had no experience with moving stimuli never developed into normal animals. In his experiments the cats were never exposed to moving objects, not even moving shadows. Their cages were illuminated by indirect lighting and the cage floors were wire, which meant that food pellets immediately dropped through them. Cats who grew up under these conditions never chased a mouse when they were older. Similarly, rats whose ability to lick themselves was reduced by means of an "Elizabethan collar" failed to show normal maternal behavior at the birth of their litters (Birch 1945).

It is thus not only the lack of—or, depending on the case— prevention of enlivening stimuli in our environment that should concern us; what is really at stake here as well is our fundamental impairment as human beings, for a person without the possibility of having *inner* experiences becomes another sort of creature. The need for stimulation of the interior world will still be present, but if it is not met, people will feel empty and dissatisfied. This is one of the reasons for the malaise, the eternal feelings of dissatisfaction, we encounter in the midst of an affluent society that floods us with stimuli. These stimuli merely express and activate a shrunken consciousness; moreover, when our vitality becomes dependent upon their constant influx, we can not free ourselves of our dependency. On the contrary, we are imperceptibly driven by our inner discontent, to whose real causes we have lost the key, more and more into the realm of externality, for there, we have learned, we can find a kind of vitality.

This type of external stimulation elicits mere reactions, never creativity; it makes us into robots. We act as if we were able to find ourselves in the things outside of us such as our possessions. We regard our life as if it were synonymous with the objects we possess, and thus our consciousness of life is reduced to what wares the market offers us. Our personality is then actually defined by the products of industry, with the result that we are motivated by desires that undoubtedly correspond not to our own needs but to those of a consumer society.

Strengthening this sort of craving or appetite is often and avidly equated with expansion of consciousness and development of the personality. In reality, however, it separates us even more from our inner malaise and emptiness, which then take the form of an obscure feeling of constant irritability which we try to relieve by new acquisitions and new external changes in our life, without recognizing our inner distress and the anger accompanying it.

Our efforts, it appears, are directed toward more and more technology and technical "fixes," for they offer us an illusion of grandiosity. But this doesn't seem to help; if we observe people, we will see how many of them rush around, throwing themselves into innumerable activities in order to flee from their undiscovered but troubling inner self, which demands its rights. Their inner self causes them anxiety, although the realization that they have this feeling and are afraid of powerlessness and helplessness is wholly lacking. Instead of anxiety they feel boredom, for instance, which only increases their frenetic activity. We often have the impression in such cases of a blind rage that is suicidal in its intensity. The research of the sociologist D. P. Phillips (1977, 1978) indicates that this is not merely a subjective reaction. In a series of articles he demonstrated that reports in the mass media of murders and suicides trigger automobile and airplane accidents; the more murders and suicides are publicized, the more frequently accidents occur on highways, as well as in private and commercial air traffic. We are led to conclude that these reports give form and impetus to such latent but diffuse destructive rages.

Our self-destructiveness will grow as long as we can "feel alive" only if guided by reactions that keep us fixated on externalities. For then we have no time for ourselves nor for our own creativity, which has to be activated for us to feel truly alive. *To be truly alive, we must feel, not merely react.* Then we will linger with things, for the creative power each of us possesses takes time to emerge and to permeate our activity. Failing this, we become robots under the sway of chains of stimuli. We become blind and lose our capacity to develop because the externality we cling to blocks the pathway to our inner self. If we should then be isolated from the stimuli customarily animating us, our mode of reaction—and along with it our personality and its cohesion—will disintegrate, unless we have developed an inner strength, an inner world.

Strangely, research into sensory deprivation stops at the point of describing the effects of isolation and gives us no information about the sole method of escaping its devastating effects. In the statistical data adduced in most of the research, no mention is made of those individuals who, even under these extreme conditions, do *not* show signs of decompensation in their personalities. To learn about them we must turn to the biographies of exceptional people and to literature.

I should like to mention two biographical examples here: Admiral Byrd, the first person to reach the South Pole, and Evelyne Bone, the English-Hungarian physician. Both were exposed to sensory deprivation, although not under experimental conditions. Byrd found himself isolated for months in an extremely monotonous polar region; his autobiography, *Alone* (1938), gives us a detailed picture of the richness of his interior life, which afforded him independence from external sensory stimulation and enabled him to overcome the complete disorientation that could otherwise have led to insanity. Bone had a similar experience (1957): she spent seven years of solitary confinement in a political prison, where the stimulation in her sensory environment was radically reduced. But thanks to her inner world of thoughts and feelings she was able to keep her mental stability and save her life. Both Evelyne Bone and Admiral Byrd were people whose personal development had created an interior world for them. That the results of research into sensory deprivation show so much mental disorder reflects on the fact that so many are without access to an inner life. The experimental results are symptomatic of the general pressure we are under today, which is driving us to become more and more dependent on external stimuli.

It is very interesting to discover in fiction something scientists cannot explain to us—or if they try, then only inadequately—about the theme under discussion. For example, in his novella *The Royal Game* (1981), which first appeared in 1943, Stefan Zweig describes a case of psychic survival under the crushing conditions of imprisonment by the Gestapo that involves almost total isolation. The hero of the story finds psychological salvation in that game of games, chess, which he plays with himself on an imaginary board.

I am not mentioning these examples in order to play down the importance of external stimulation but to direct attention to a situation which otherwise we are almost unconscious of: under the conditions we more and more have been exposed to in our development, we are increasingly influenced by those stimuli that do not touch our inner self and consequently make us more dependent on the external world. This may foster the illusion that we are in possession of our self, but in fact, by seeking out the influx of external stimuli which do not produce any inner reactions, we are only reinforcing our dependency on them. This vicious circle—in the end a frenetic search for change itself—has a destructive effect, since it is basically this addiction that makes it impossible for us to recognize our true needs. We will be ruled by the appetites created by external pressures, and because our inner self remains untouched and unsatisfied, it will be a source of malaise that breeds rage and destructiveness.

And it will be difficult to find a path leading back to ourselves. We need teachers—only we do not realize it. For in our formative environment each of us acts in accordance with the selfsame model: a frenzied, outward-directed search. We are not in a position to acknowledge our own traumas, the loss of access to our own needs and feelings. What we have here is the death of human experience! Our reality has become unreal, since by now we can deal with ourselves only in terms of abstract concepts determined from outside. Our true needs are unknown to us and are lost from sight.

Surrounded by dead possessions and by change for its own sake, we keep on running in place. The more change we seek in the external world—the more often we replace our clothes and change our location, our automobile, our gadgets—the more intolerant we become of the uncertainty we're exposed to on a daily basis. This seems to be a paradox until we realize that our frenzy for what is new comes from fear, from a fear of coming into contact with our inner feelings from which we are kept at a distance and which thus must strike us as alien and dangerous. They constitute the new insecurity which appears to oppress us. Still, only if we can succeed in establishing contact with our inner feelings once again, will we find a pathway leading out of our plight.

In this connection there is something we must not forget: humor is an important element of life. We need it not only because it helps us get through life's troubles but because it also makes us feel more alive. Without it we are dead, and, as a matter of fact, those of us without a sense of humor are the ones who always strike us as dead or deadly. But in the realm of humor too an increasing diminution is taking place.

If we compare today's film comedies with those of the past, we will note that something has changed, that something is missing. Although the recent films generally display technical mastery, their content, even if it makes us laugh, leaves us with a feeling of emptiness.

Let us look, for purposes of contrast, at an old Marx Brothers movie: The scene opens with Groucho's arrival in America from an African safari. He is seated in an elegant sedan chair borne by natives dressed in full war regalia. When they set him down in New York, he asks the chief, "How much?" The chief answers, "Twenty-one dollars." Groucho, reproachfully: "But I told you not to take me via Australia!" In another movie, Groucho is in a train station in New York buying a ticket to California. The clerk at the window tells him it will cost $116, whereupon Groucho hands him a wad of bills, saying, "You don't have to count them." Of course the clerk does count them and reports that sixteen dollars are missing. Groucho, indignantly: "I told you not to count them!"

Why are these old comedies more than just pleasant memories? Somehow they activate something in us, awaken something that addresses our own inner experience. The more recent comedies, on the other hand, appear to act as stimuli that produce direct reactions without setting any meaningful inner processes in motion. These reactions are robotlike; any inner empathy is missing, and as a result something fundamental is lost.

I once went to see a double feature: an old Marx Brothers film followed by a comedy of the modern type. The audience, predominantly young people, didn't know what to make of the older film, but during the second one they roared with laughter at scenes that were filled with words like "fuck" and "shit." The dramatic context was minimal; it seemed as if the words themselves with their antisocial connotations were releasing pent-up rage by means of raucous laughter. They served simply to trigger the rage produced by a diminished world. In this sense, the reaction was "preformed."

In order to enjoy the Marx Brothers film one needs an inner feeling of aliveness, a creative reaction of one's own. The young people apparently had no access to their inner self; if they did, they aggressively resisted being reminded of it by showing demonstrative signs of boredom.

Movies are naturally not all that has changed in our world; a general change in our relationship to our feelings and our creative powers can be observed everywhere. If our genuine feelings and our creativity are not nurtured, then they will gradually become deadened and we will be impoverished. The emptiness that develops in us as a result makes us furious, all the more so since the malaise it engenders is threatening to us and increases our potential for destructiveness.

When we are moved to participate in a work of art, when a film touches us inwardly, we learn—even without words—something about ourselves. But to an increasing extent we are being exposed to a world that makes it impossible for us to know our inner selves. Our lives are becoming a series of preformed reactions instead of perceived experiences, and the rapid-fire constant change is becoming a substitute for feelings. We have no chance to linger with ourselves, to ponder over things; everything is presented to us for instant consumption in "bite-size" portions that are often predigested as well. Thus, we are no longer accustomed to experiencing *suspense as a spur to our own actions..*

Our dependence on this one-sided type of stimulation is increasing daily. Many people can't even walk around any more without having their transistor radio turned on. Either they can't bear their own emotions or they can't endure the feeling of emptiness that sets in the moment there are no external stimuli to maintain their artificially induced sense of vitality. It is important to emphasize that because we have appropriated this sort of stimulus-world and its values, we consider ourselves to be autonomous, without noticing at all that Orwell's *1984* is already upon us. The shocking thing is that the situation described in his famous novel is not to be found only in dictatorial regimes of terror but also to a high degree where official violence is not apparent.

The separation from our true self also influences the way we regard our personal history. More and more frequently people act as if their past were without significance for their present life.

I am reminded of the attitude expressed by a student of mine at Rutgers University. I had been speaking about the American dramatist William Hanley and his play *Slow Dance on the Killing Ground* (1964), a masterful work about three characters who all have a frightful, traumatic life behind them but, with the exception of one, lack feelings that are commensurate with the nature of their past. Rosie, a modern college girl, intellectual and cut off from her feelings, is on her way to have an abortion, which means no more to her than slicing a piece of salami. Glas, a former German Communist, is able to erase the horror of having abandoned his wife to the Nazis by his devotion to an ideology. Only Randall, who has murdered his mother because her prostitution wounded him so deeply, is consciously appalled at what he has done.

My psychology student remarked that she didn't see why it was of any particular significance to have a mother who was a prostitute. "Social amnesia" (as Russell Jacoby called it in 1975) surrounds us; it is the deliberate repression of things we once knew about but then became afraid of, with the result that we repress both the fear and the situation giving rise to it.

I would like, after this digression, to return to the theme of humor. Without some connection with our past we can not really laugh at ourselves; humor presupposes that we have a vital contact with our own history.

In the film *International Hotel* we see the comedian W. C. Fields flying cheerfully through the clouds in a kind of precursor of the helicopter when he suddenly notices that his supply of beer is running out. He lands on the roof of the International Hotel somewhere in China, where the city's elite are drinking afternoon tea. In a resounding, but at the same time, slightly quavering voice Fields asks where he is. "Wu Hu," comes the polite reply. "I'm looking for Kansas City, Kansas," he cries in helpless indignation. "You are lost, Sir!" a voice squeaks. Whereupon Fields, mocking the self-centered certainty of those without a real center, draws himself up to his full height, throws out his chest and bellows, "Kansas City is lost; *I* am here!"

The point is that those who have never experienced their inner self, who have never been truly alive, are also unable to laugh at the idea that they might have no center of their own.

V

Patients in Psychotherapy

M OST cultures[1] must be regarded as instruments for producing and maintaining splits in human consciousness. If we wish to describe and analyze a civilization, we should ask ourselves the following question: To what extent does the civilization (or culture) prevent children from becoming aware of the suppression of their autonomy? How does it stop them from becoming conscious of the true sources of their helplessness and rage? How does culture manage to turn this rage and the resulting destructive drive into a type of attitude that denies the human need for love and sympathy, making people insensitive to these emotions?

Questions like these bring us face to face with the phenomenon of splitting off and estrangement in a given culture, and—odd as it may seem—if we keep these issues in mind, it will soon become apparent which cultures bear within them the seeds of death and destructive hatred and which are truly allied with life. Such questions arise out of an orientation that regards a "well-adjusted" life as the end product of a development based on the fragmentation of consciousness. Posing them will help us solve the mystery of psychic illness. To do this we need a broad perspective that takes into full account the total relationship of the culture to the development of the individual. This will then reveal to us the real meaning of psychological "illness": people who are unable to live with a split as the basic structure of their personality become "ill."

Those among us who still retain their sensitivity, who still long for another shore[2] of sensibility—in other words, those who still believe in the possibility of loving another person in complete consciousness of that person's individuality and who still desire to be loved in the same way themselves—must pay a price. They often feel alienated, suffer without knowing why, and are full of anxiety. They may become failures in their life or work. In one way or another, they become outsiders.

Some of these people, from the very beginning of their development, are unable to live with the split that is demanded by their culture; others aren't troubled by it until that moment when they are suddenly confronted with feelings they apparently have never experienced before and therefore cannot deal with. This is why we see two basic categories of patients in psychotherapy: those who "always" have had difficulties in life and those who "suddenly" break down, seemingly out of the clear blue sky. This is not to say that everyone who fits these two descriptions is in psychotherapy or should be. Many have sufficient energy, as well as friends or a partner, to help them find the way to their self.

The first category of patients has always had difficulty accepting the ways and means provided by their culture for "sublimating" helplessness and anger, that is, obedience, conformity, suppression of intense feelings, and command of various techniques. From an early age, such people cannot tolerate a life-style shaped by the manifold forms of domination and compulsion. They never submit completely to society's pressure to split apart their feelings. The strength of their perceptions contradicts the cultural lie that claims their autonomy has been suppressed out of love. They become ill because they have refused, without necessarily being aware of what they are doing, to go along with such a self-deceptive arrangement. Their protest and refusal, however, often do not appear on the surface, for they are intimidated by their own rage. This adds to their fear of their actual oppressors, whose "love" they so needed as children. Consequently, they are not only afraid of their own aggressiveness but also believe that they are evil. Their rebellion therefore usually expresses itself by their becoming a failure in life.

Many of these patients come to us with the desperate "hope" that their plight is really their own fault. They want therapy to make them like the rest of us: well-adjusted, obedient, successful, and with the freedom to act in a destructive way like other people. Some patients, however, really want to get to the root of things but are perplexed over how to go about it. The first type, once they are freed of their guilt feelings, can readily be made into successful, ambitious, adjusted, and insensitive or inconsiderate members of society. The second type causes more trouble for the psychotherapist or psychoanalyst. They are often regarded as "borderline cases," as too ill to be helped—if, that is, their therapist doesn't accept their constant complaint, often expressed in a disguised obscure, and totally inappropriate form, that something is wrong with the outside world. I personally find these patients the most promising to work with.

The second category, consisting of those who suddenly find themselves confronted with feelings their split consciousness—which is officially sanctioned and culturally conditioned—has made them shun, can also be divided into two groups. Those in the first group want nothing other than to be returned to a state of non-feeling, of insensitivity; whereas those in the second would like to use their crisis as an opportunity to overcome their split. The first group comprises the favorite patients of psychotherapists and psychiatrists who work primarily with mind-altering drugs, shock treatment, systematic behavior modification, and sometimes also with certain varieties of group therapy. They attempt to "help" paitents get rid of their deeply troubling feelings. The second group, on the other hand, can become true fighters, who take advantage of their breakdown to achieve self-integration on a lasting basis. (In the strength of their motivation—not in the type of their previous adaptation—they often resemble the "borderline cases" of the first category.)

The latter kind of patient is exemplified by a forty-year-old, energetic, successful businesswoman who entered therapy with me. Several months earlier, she had met a man who gave her the feeling that he was taking care of her, being supportive and comforting. For the first time in her life, she felt that a burden had been lifted from her shoulders; but as soon as she began to react spontaneously, to let her partner know what her needs were, he withdrew. Since he was the one who had activated these needs in her, she believed that her fate lay in his hands; without him, her life suddenly seemed meaningless.

This patient had lived her whole life without experiencing real love. Her mother's cool interest was the only "love" she had known. But when her long-repressed fantasy of receiving genuine support from an unknown father was stimulated and brought to life by her new admirer, she felt completely at the mercy of those feelings she had held in check her whole life by being "strong," efficient, independent, and successful. Since society found these qualities good and worthwhile, they gave stability to her self-image. The split in her consciousness that made it possible for her not to come to terms with the fact of having been wounded by an unempathic mother was also the impetus behind her drive to be successful, independent, and strong.

But from the moment her need for warmth, for being taken care of, was awakened, no matter how unrealistic and futile her hope that her needs would now be met, her strength seemed to evaporate. Her self-image, which had been held together by splitting off and denial, fell apart on both a psychic and somatic level, with high blood pressure being one of her more serious physical symptoms. The patient, however, did not want to use tranquillizers to solve her problems; she had sensed in herself "another shore" that held a promise of other worlds, and her physician supported her attitude. For this woman, psychotherapy led to discovery of her self: she found out that her fear of being alone, the way she was clinging to her friend, was essentially a manifestation of her fear of having a self of her own. Her "strength" and "independence," attributes so impressive to herself and others, turned out to be her way of responding to the expectations and demands of her mother and of her environment. Her own vitality and aliveness lay hidden deep within her.

When her hitherto buried needs finally resurfaced, she clung to a man who, exactly like her mother, was deeply afraid of these needs. The anxiety triggered by such a situation is a way of attempting to reject new possibilities of discovering a vital self. Reexperiencing early feelings brings back the fear of becoming involved in the growth of a self of one's own. This is why being alone then becomes unbearable: one absolutely needs another person in order to be able to avoid the now real possibility of experiencing one's self and the accompanying anxiety that dates back to earliest childhood.

Many peole cling to each other to escape their self. This woman, however, had the courage to rediscover herself and her sensitivity, to alter that part of herself which had been so obsessed by the external world—for example, by financial success.

Psychotherapies differ profoundly on this question: some lend support to the culture's propensity for splitting off, while others search for the individual's full truth and a genuine relationship to the world. In the last analysis, every form of psychotherapy is a moral enterprise, since the evil in human beings is caused by the fact that many people are unable to deal with the experiences of their childhood and youth that led to splits in their personality. The moral choice before psychotherapy, then, is whether it *ought* to help patients find the strength to integrate those painful experiences or, instead, serve as a subtle means of helping them continue in their self-denial, of helping them repress again that sensitivity which brought them to the point of rebelling—even if they were not aware of doing so. In part, as in the case discussed above, the choice is up to the patient. In any event, there is an inescapable connection between the patient's "illness" and a sensitivity which gives him or her no peace.

Should therapists endeavor to silence this sensitivity? Wouldn't they then be betraying the truth? And if they do, is it for the sake of protecting the patient or because of their own identification with the powers that be and their own complicity in the splitting off sanctioned by their culture?

How else could a psychoanalytic author such as Michael Maccoby, who describes today's heroes in his book *The New Bosses* (1976) as actually measuring their virility by the distance from which they can urinate against a tree or by the degree to which they act like male chauvinists, fail to notice the extent to which these and other similar attitudes and forms of behavior are an expression of megalomania or, in any case, a kind of madness? Maccoby reports these behavior patterns among circles of leading, highly regarded managers, viewing all this as perfectly normal. How much is he being taken in here by his own identification with success and power? In my opinion, he is confusing the *absence* of anxiety with psychological health.

The crucial point here is that *people who permit themselves to have feelings are also exposing themselves to feelings of anxiety*. Fantasies of power, on the other hand, protect us from anxiety as well as from all other subtle and sensitive feelings—at least until the repressed feelings surface unexpectedly. Maccoby's attitude is an example of a remarkable splitting off and disintegration of feelings, or put differently: only those feelings are permitted here that serve an artificial identity, one based exclusively on power.

Our patients' suffering is caused specifically by the fact that their identification with power estranges them from their own self. In spite of this identification, all of us, even those who are well adjusted, still have a fear of being hurt, of having to think of themselves as "weak" because they are afraid of being overpowered by their need for another person. Since their suffering is conscious, they do have some knowledge of these fears.

In the following pages I shall demonstrate what a confusing undertaking it is—given the conditions existing in our culture—to attempt to integrate our varied and contradictory experiences. Since our cultural patterns mainly offer control, domination, and power as cures (we really ought to say, as painkillers), they block a truly curative process that could reverse our condition of disintegration.

I had a patient who was a forceful, vital, and ebullient woman. One day she came to a session in a fury, which she tried her best to conceal. She had scarcely sat down when she told me how much she trusted me. I felt the opposite to be true and finally asked if she was angry or afraid.

She looked up in surprise: "Angry? Yes, I know anger, but fear?"

Then she blurted out: "I will not be dominated! I must do my own thing!"

I wondered why it was that part of her wanted to confide in me, while another part was unable to share with another person.

I asked her about this, and she replied, "I don't know. I won't give in."

I said, "It sounds as if you have to fight me." For I felt she was struggling against her own need to be trusting because she saw this as weakness. I then told her my feeling was that she sounded exactly the way she had told me her mother was: shrill, icy, and contemptuous. All of a sudden her demeanor changed; she looked straight at me for the first time that day and said sadly, "That's terrible."

But it was true. By being as nasty and cold as her mother—and in that way also saying no to the husband who loved her—she was being loyal to her mother and justifying the latter's behavior. She was thus reinforcing the split, the denial of her emotions, for which her mother was responsible. By repeating her mother's pattern, she was not being herself.

"I hold back, just to be rotten."

"Yes," I countered. "You're taking her part. You could stop doing it, but then you would feel anxious."

She said, "That rings true—but why?"

"We'll see," I responded.

After a while: "Really, I don't trust any man, you included. Mother never trusted a man either. It's not love for her, but I do believe she relied on me. It means I was the only one she could turn to."

This is the way parents get children to be exactly the way they want them and in the process cripple their children's self. The mother's ploy in this case was to give her little Mary a feeling of importance, while actually controlling her. It was a seductive trick to let Mary feel she had "power" over her mother, whereas the truth of their relationship was just the opposite.

And then all the rest unravelled itself during that session: the many arrangements we make and the everyday ways we keep repeating the myths that in reality undo us yet seem to prop us up with a self-esteem based on triumphing over others.

"That's it! Wait, there's a connection with Doris [her husband's ex-wife]—some kind of fantasy—don't know—it's coming to me—can't quite get it. There's a connection between her and mother. They're alike. I feel like Peter Pan [who never wanted to grow up]. I guess I feel victorious—I feel I'm better than she is."

I: "Why victorious? Why is that so important? Why make a triumph out of feeling you're a person in your own right? Making it a triumph *is* your connection to your mother."

"Wait, I had thought of writing a story." Mary's story, it turned out, revolved around incidents that justified her mother's contempt for her family.

"The meaning of your story," I said to Mary, "was—and still is—that you thought your mother was right to feel superior; that signified for you *that others were considerably worse than she*, which made her less bad in your eyes—and that saved you from your despair about her. But what you have here is a hollow triumph. True, the others *were* worse, but what remained unsaid was *that you are all one of a kind*, and so you're not free to separate yourself from them. It's not a question of triumph. *You are different*; there is no connection between you and her and the others."

A long pause followed; then: "Ha! What a revelation it is that I'm different—I never wanted to be —wanted to get lost in a crowd of fat women. I *am* different, but maybe I don't want to be!"

But she was. She had fought courageously against her past without knowing it—at first in a self-destructive way when she married her first husband: by taking care of her yet at the same time finding fault with her, he confirmed her contempt for herself and all women. Still, she kept struggling to cope with her life. She did her best for her children, made every effort to be creative by writing and painting, which she was even able to enjoy some of the time.

"I suddenly feel such a surge of love for John [her present husband]. If I really am different, then I can love him! You know, feeling different makes me anxious and fearful. What shall I do?"

"Learn to live with it. You thought your mother was strong because she never seemed anxious. She was just denying her anxiety, pushing it aside as a sign of weakness; she had nothing but contempt for what constitutes our humanity."

"Yes, I always used to think of her as gigantic."

But the fear of being herself persisted for Mary, as it does for all of us. In the next session she talked about her accomplishments. She had articles appearing simultaneously in several magazines. But as she told me about this, she didn't give me the impression of being sure of herself at all.

"When I got home yesterday I kissed John again and again. It had to do with what we talked about in the last hour, about me being different. I know and yet I don't know what we're talking about."

"What will die," I asked, "if you let go of someone?" I meant her mother.

"I will—my mother always struck me as a live wire. Vitality personified."

That was true; without a doubt, her mother was vital. I pursued my line of questioning: "What is it that you are so terrified of?"

She: "I had fantasies of being without John. It was terrifying. Who will look out for me if I'm all alone? That has something to do with mother, something would disintegrate—something that's buried under slime! Ugh! Maybe if I let go—it sounds nutty—I would have nothing left to justify what is dirty in me. [She was referring to connections that had emerged in previous sessions: if I'm no longer like my mother, then I have to take responsibility for being a different person from her, for then I would be in tune with my own feelings.] I've done it! I didn't know that! There it is, once and for all. *What do I do now?* Oh, the old silver cord, the umbilical cord."

She understood that her question was a form of repetition insofar as she was behaving toward me *as if* she belonged to her mother (or to me or to someone else) and not to herself.

"And when John says he doesn't know what he did to deserve me, he makes me feel so responsible. Oh, that's it; I almost forgot: to justify myself, I cling to mother because her dirt justifies mine. It's as though my whole life has suddenly become clear to me —I almost fooled myself completely."

Here we see why many of us are often so angry. To be the way we really could be, to be no less human than other people, would mean experiencing fear and sometimes feeling full of anxiety. And we would be acting contrary to what we learned in early life, for to be *less* than the authorities around us (e.g., our parents), to make ourselves—and permit ourselves to be made—small, is a method many of us use to placate and pacify the powers that be. Giving up such a defense mechanism understandably creates fear and malaise. That is why we become so angry at whatever challenges us to change.

The paradox of what we call psychopathology is that people become ill because they have retained a sensitivity that contradicts the "reality" of the split world they are exposed to, while at the same time identifying with this world which is so oppressive to them. As a result, they become split themselves, and what they find threatening is then internalized. That is why many believe that their suffering would be cured if only they were as powerful as those who wounded them in the first place.

The people who strike us as the most disturbed, the schizophrenics, are the most radical opponents of this type of identification, for they attempt to withdraw completely from our world. They are accordingly regarded as *dissociated*, since such an act of disidentification entails a split between affect and the socially accepted significance of nascent human relationships. In cases where others use pity as a weapon in order to feel superior or to oppress another person, schizophrenics are unable to feel compassion. They may laugh when we, who go along with the game, expect the "compassionate" reactions of kindness or grief. By means of disidentification they refuse to participate in this socially sanctioned form of behavior. Therefore, they don't live in our reality; they are or once were aware of it, however, although they approach it with what seem to us to be totally inappropriate notions. Two things are true of them: they are closer to the truth and at the same time estranged from reality.

It is important to distinguish the split condition of schizophrenics from the split in consciousness caused by the numerous forms of false love. The latter split distorts or even makes impossible our self-perception, our view of ourselves, and any appropriate reaction to relationships involving oppression and love. An essential aspect of the so-called split in schizophrenics, on the other hand, is their realization of the true state of affairs, although they are unable to express in realistic terms what has often been impressed upon them at a preverbal stage. They see the hypocrisy of a love that isn't love at all but don't have the strength or ability to live with this truth in a schizoid world.

They don't realize that their own truth could be a source of strength to them, for this truth was discredited at too early an age. That is their fundamental trauma. Recognizing the hypocrisy of a love that loves nothing but submissiveness, they are constantly trying to prove that they can't be loved by such a world, even going to the extent of making themselves as unlovable as possible. A living death is the result of this radical and subjective form of truthfulness. Such truthfulness, in turn, makes it possible to work with them in direct and honest ways.

VI

The Search for the Self and Its Betrayal

CONTRARY to popular and scholarly belief, humaneness does not depend on the degree of intellectual sophistication a given culture has attained, nor is it the product of giving thought to moral values. Morality derives from forces more vital than any scheme of thinking imposed upon human beings. Whenever morality is based on external considerations, we will find the preconditions for every kind of nonmorality and, ultimately, inhumanity. The supposed primitiveness of our forebears and of other peoples is a myth we use to cover up our own moral defects. In this sense, there are no primitive peoples, only human beings who are impaired in their humaneness.

A self that is firmly grounded in autonomy can not live with destructiveness. Destructiveness is something that develops in people; it is not innate but requires a complex process of growth, marked by the failure to attain autonomy. Underlying destructiveness, there is a split in the psyche: a baby of only one month already shows signs of suffering when its unitary perception of the mother is interfered with.[1]

When adjustment to social reality demands a splitting in the psyche and makes this a guiding principle of development, people become evil. Then they will constantly try to regain possession of that part of the self they have lost by seeking it *outside of themselves*. The expression of such a search may have society's approval (as in the case of wars fought in the name of an ideology, a god, or some "moral" conviction), or it may take an undisguisedly criminal form. Behind both forms of expression is a desire, developed early, to conquer something internal by means of an external possession.

The German author Jakob Wassermann illustrates this situation in his portrait of the murderer Niels Heinrich in the novel *The World's Illusion* (1920). He shows us a man who in his implacable hatred for everything that is living and good finally even murders a pure and loving girl, thereby taking his revenge and expressing his contempt for the hypocrisy his life is built on. By this act he also gives vent to the anger he feels for needing that part of his psyche he has lost— that loving part from which he has been cut off. Heinrich provides an unvarnished example of the attempt to seize by force something in the external world that is lacking in the internal one and in this way to compensate for the void within:

If he, Niels Heinrich, could work his will, there wouldn't be one stone left standing on another, all rules would be wiped out, all order destroyed, all cities blown up sky-high, all wells choked, all bridges broken, all books burned, all roads torn up, and destruction would be preached, and war—war of each against all, all against each, all against all. Mankind wasn't worthy of nothing [sic] better.

He could truthfully say that because he had studied people and had seen through them. He had seen nothing but liars and thieves, wretched fools, misers, and the meanly ambitious. He had seen the dogs cringe and creep when they wanted to rise, cringe before those above, snap at those below. He knew the rich with their full bellies and their rotten phrases, and the poor with their contemptible patience. He knew the bribe-takers and the stiff-necked ones, and the braggarts and the slinkers, the thieves and forgers, ladies' men and cowards, the harlots and their procurers, the respectable women with their hypocrisy and envy, their pretense and masquerade and play-acting; he knew it all, and it couldn't impress him no [sic] more. And there were no real things in the world except stench and misery and avarice and greed and treachery and malevolence and lust. The world was a loathsome thing and had to be destroyed. And any one who had come to see that must take the last step, the vary last, to the place where despair and contempt are self-throttled, where you could go no further, where you hear the Angel of the Last Day beating at the dull walls of the flesh, whither neither the light penetrated nor the darkness, but where one was alone with one's rage and could feel oneself utterly, and heighten that self and take something sacred and smash it into bits. That was it, that! To take something holy, something pure, and become master of it and grind it to the earth and stamp it out. (Vol. 2, pp. 344–45)

Wassermann demonstrates here how rage alone can still give a split person a sense of aliveness. The dreadful paradox lies in the fact that his destructiveness is the source of his vitality. That is a terrible state of affairs but one we encounter daily in one form or another, since people like Heinrich—who are to be found on all levels of society—can't live without being destructive.

Thanks to their ability to adjust to socially approved patterns of behavior, people without a genuine self all too often give the appearance of having normal and acceptable feelings. Because they are actually cut off from all feelings except revenge directed at whatever is alive and vital, they seem to be free of fear, anxiety, and tension. This impresses someone who is unable to bear his or her own anxieties and tensions, with the consequence that such people are admired, especially if they are highly ambitious.

We fail to recognize one of the main aspects of Nazism if we regard it only as a uniquely German aberration that does not apply to the rest of us. What led to the success of the National Socialists and their power structure was not only their virulent anti-Semitism and open criminality: it was "the new man" that came into ascendency with them, a man without personhood, without a self.

The degree to which this was true is dramatically illustrated by a telling detail of Adolf Eichmann's behavior. In a television interview, one of his abductors reported that when Eichmann had to move his bowels, he sat down on the toilet and then obediently asked his guard, "May I do it now?" He gave the other person, the one who now had power over him, control over his most private bodily functions!

The horrifying aspect of the "banality of evil" (to use Hannah Arendt's phrase) doesn't lie in a person's ordinariness, but in the masses of people without a self who seem to us to be human beings with human feelings and are also held up to us as such. Hans Frank, Governor General of the Nazi Protectorate of Poland, made a statement to G. N. Gilbert, the American court psychologist at the Nuremberg trials, that shows us just what kind of feelings are actually involved here. Frank called Hitler a seducer and continued in these words:

> You know, the people are really feminine . . . so emotional, so fickle, so dependent on mood and environment, so suggestible . . . so ready to obey . . . .[It's not only that they're obedient; they're ready to] surrender, like a woman. . . . After he had led us on and set the whole world in motion, he simply disappeared—deserted us, and left us to take the blame for everything that happened. . . . There must be some basic evil in me—in all men. . . . Mass hypnosis—that hardly explains it. Ambition, that had a lot to do with it. Just imagine. I was a minister at thirty; rode about in a limousine, had servants. . . . For a moment you are intoxicated . . . then . . . you open your hand, and it is empty—utterly empty. (Manvell and Fraenkel 1967, pp. 127–28)

Like Albert Speer, Hitler's architect and Minister of Armaments and one of Frank's codefendants, Frank appeared to be normal, emotional, humble, willing to confront himself, and intelligent. I mention Speer, who was active mainly in the area of industry, because he resembles the organizational wizards of our own contemporary society: friendly, a genius at sensing where agreement and manipulation are possible, elegant, and devoted to an apparently impersonal goal of greatness; he was essentially suited for *everything*—hence amoral and, in spite of his brilliant social exterior, lacking any inner identity.[2]

What actually lies behind that seemingly candid and sincere observation that "people are really feminine . . . so ready to . . . surrender, like a woman"? Nothing other than scorn for women because they surrender themselves to men! And this is uttered by someone who of course demands surrender from women, someone who possesses no self outside of his devotion to success. Here we see the consequence of an attitude that is perpetuated when one person's autonomy is surrendered to another's will. In all probability the reason why such men scorn and despise feminine qualities is because they secretly despise *themselves* for the surrender of their self, but they project their scorn onto women, from whom they demand the same thing!

Yet this is the kind of self that flourishes today among the political, economic, and even scientific leaders of our society, who, to be sure, don't exhibit the undisguised bloodthirstiness of Hitler and his cohorts but are no less dangerous on that account.[3] Perhaps they are even more so, since their lack of self is not immediately discernible behind their camouflage of normality, success, service, and apparent devotion to moral standards.

The antidote against evil is not conscience. Guilt feelings, which themselves often play a role in distorting development, simply contribute to the preconditions for a profound destructivity. Real change comes about only if we learn to deal with the fear behind our untiring search for an irreal security. Only if we undertake the painful process of bringing our fears to consciousness will we be able to open our hearts and increase our sensitivity to our fellow human beings. Søren Kierkegaard wrote in 1849, "The opposite of sin is not virtue but faith." This means faith in the possibility of creating for ourselves a self that is grounded in truth.

This is anything but easy, and many of us shun the effort involved because we believe what we have been promised: that if we will only be obedient, our life will be free of conflict. A patient of mine attempted to live according to this rule by being "sweet," "nice," and "docile" all her life until one day she was forced to confront an unforeseen experience.

This thirty-year-old woman had spent her childhood and youth under conditions of extreme exploitation and violence. When she was ten, for example, she complained to her mother that a roomer was molesting her sexually, whereupon her mother responded by saying, "If you want me to throw him out, come up with his rent money first." As long as she was submissive, she was able to go on living with her situation, but any questioning about herself and her mother was nipped in the bud. With great effort, she finished high school, and then at twenty-six went on to study social work.

In the course of her studies, she visited a hospital as part of a seminar she was taking; there she suddenly found herself in the same unit where she had spent nearly three months following surgery when she was eight years old. This unforeseen reencounter caused all the rage she had repressed on that occasion to come crashing down on her. But at the very moment she became conscious of the anger she had felt toward her doctors and nurses, who had shown no feeling or understanding for the little girl, she heard an internalized cultural command: *Don't feel sorry for yourself!* That was exactly the way her mother (and her social milieu) used to react to her perception and experience of violence and pain caused by authority figures. Therefore, the patient immediately dismissed her own feelings and participated in the seminar as though nothing had happened. But her rage had stimulated guilt feelings and self-hatred and made her feel that she was not well-enough adjusted. Her predicament was that she had to be dishonest and false toward herself if she was to reap that reward—so crucial for her—which was conditional upon her observing the rules. Her success at this then won the benevolent approval of all those in authority.

Fortunately, the patient had not repressed her feelings completely. She was still open enough to suddenly see through the cruel principle her fellow students followed in selecting children for therapy. She sensed their dishonesty and hypocrisy when she realized that the children, who all came from the lowest social class, were chosen not on the basis of the urgency of their problems but according to their usefulness in terms of the topic of a student's seminar paper. Only if the results were "good" would the student receive a high grade and/or a favorable recommendation from the professor. Because of this, children became objects whose needs and distress were being manipulated for the sake of a grade.

It was agonizing for the young woman each time she had to

select one child at the expense of another. For the other students her deep dilemma was simply a sign of stupidity and maladjustment. By not acknowledging her genuine human nature, they were also able to keep their own human feelings from surfacing.

The complexity of the problem for the patient is indicated by the fact that she wanted to go along with the others but was able to do so only by "betraying" her truth. How was she to resolve these contradictions?

Her need to be "sweet" and her inability to asssimilate her rage were expressed in the following dream sequence: she was in front of a mirror but was afraid to look into it, for the reflection was not of herself but of a wild and furious "she," who might harm the good "she." She tried to wipe away the image in the mirror but then grew frightened and confused because that would mean erasing herself. This dream made her aware of the split in her personality and of her lifelong attempt to maintain this split. Now she realized that rubbing away the "bad" image would destroy a fundamental and vital part of herself, and she didn't want to do that.

The struggle for a self of one's own gives some people the strength to preserve both their self and their contact with a societal reality that is actually *un*real on many levels. Out of such a struggle comes also pleasure in one's own aliveness and that of others.

Since the kind of self that is involved here is not an abstract image but represents a state of solidarity with one's own feelings, as well as those of others, it can exist only as long as the struggle for such solidarity remains alive. The continuity of the self is therefore predicated on an ongoing renewal of these connections, along with the suffering, joy, and ecstasy that accompany them. That is why aliveness is flux, why stability involves the capacity to tolerate tension, and why no individual can completely avoid succumbing to the attraction of the promise of a conflict-free existence.

AFTERWORD

GEORGE Orwell in his *Collected Essays* (1968) has described the heart of that experience which gives rise to a child's feeling of helplessness and despair. In a memoir he tells us that he had just been beaten by the headmaster of his boarding school:

> . . . I was not even now crying because of the pain. The second beating had not hurt very much either. Fright and shame seemed to have anesthetized me. I was crying partly because I felt that this was expected of me, partly from genuine repentance, but partly also because of a deeper grief which is peculiar to childhood and not easy to convey: *a sense of desolate loneliness and helplessness, of being locked up not only in a hostile world but in a world of good and evil where the rules were such that it was actually not possible for me to keep them.* (Orwell's italics.) (p. 382)

Despair such as this has the effect of making our inner self alien to us, regardless of whether our personality develops in the direction of rebellion or of adjustment to norms. We will subsequently cling to outer forms whether they are those of society's official ideology or of an opposing one. It is because we are alienated from our inner world—which causes it to appear to us as formless and anarchistic and hence threatening—that we cling so firmly to these external forms in the hope of preserving a sense of our own identity.

Franz Kafka portrays this futile clinging to externalities with great empathy. In Kafka's novel *The Trial*, for instance, Joseph K. attempts to prove who he is—by means of his bicycle license! Kafka's heroes suffer because they have vainly placed their faith in an inadequate external identity. They hope to achieve integration by adherence to "patriarchal" law, to protect themselves in this way from the disintegration threatened by their own apparent formlessness—but again this is in vain. How different the case is for the heroes of B. Traven's novels, for Koslowski in *The Death Ship*, for example, who struggles to the very end against having an identity imposed upon him.

The distinction between rebellion and adjustment is a fundamental one. Only rebellion makes authenticity possible, but it must lead to a sense of community with our fellow human beings. If it is directed only *against* something, it becomes an end in itself and results in an overemphasis of one's own importance. This amounts to a rejection of the search for the true self and eventually produces a self without a heart. The dangers here are not the external ones the individual encounters but fear of the terrors of loneliness and fear of chaos and insanity.

When inner transformation fails to accompany rebellion directed against the external world, the outcome is the same as to adjustment. Since Henry Miller, himself a great rebel, informs us so cogently about this in his study of the failure of Rimbaud's rebellion, I should like to return to his discussion here.

The life of Rimbaud, short but feverish—he completed his greatest work, *A Season in Hell*, when he was eighteen—is the story of a man who revolted against conformity and rigidity and then, after he had succeeded with great effort in expanding his freedom and his level of consciousness, turned around and opted for financial security. Beginning with an extraordinary attempt to explore "the wonders of the earth," he severed himself as a youth from friends and relatives to experience life in all its fullness. But suddenly he, who as a young man had found "the disorder of his mind sacred," completely renounced his unique life of defiance; his search for authenticity came to a standstill, he made an about face and proceeded from then on in the opposite direction. He became like the enemy he had hated.

As a youth, Miller writes, Rimbaud ran away from the unbearable provincial atmosphere of his home; later, out of terror or out of fear of madness, he went over to the side of the powers that rule the world and began to trade in gold, rifles, and slaves.

"He surrendered his treasure," says Miller, "as if *it* were the burden."

> During the "Night in Hell," when he realizes that he is the slave of his baptism, he cries: "O Parents, you contrived my misfortune, and your own." . . . He renounces everything which would link him with the age or the land he was born in. "I am ready for perfection," he states. And he was, in a sense. He had prepared his own initiation, survived the terrible ordeal, and then relapsed into the night in which he was born. He had perceived that there was a step beyond art, he had put his foot over the threshold, and then in terror or in fear of madness he had retreated. . . . One has to come to the end of one's forces, learn that one *is* a slave—in whatever realm—in order to desire emancipation. The perverse, negative will fostered by one's parents has to be made submissive before it can become positive and integrated with the heart and mind. The Father (in all his guises)[1] has to be dethroned so that the Son may reign. . . . He is the stern taskmaster, the dead letter of the Law, the *Verboten* sign. One kicks the traces over, goes berserk, filled with a false power and a foolish pride. And then one breaks, and the I that is not the I surrenders. *But Rimbaud did not break.* He does not dethrone the father, he identifies himself with him. . . . He goes over into the opposite, becomes the very enemy whom he hated. . . . He changes identity so thoroughly that if he were to pass himself on the road he would not recognize himself. This is perhaps the last desperate way of tricking madness—to become so utterly sane that one does not know one is insane." (Miller 1956, p. 101ff.)

At the end of his life, as "he tormentedly inched his way towards death on the farm of his miserly mother," he snapped at someone who tried to ask him some questions about the poetry of his early days, " 'Please cut it out! I'm *through* with all that shit' " (Rimbaud 1979, p. 14). It was as if he were trying to erase the hated outlines of his rebellious self.

This profound insight into the insanity of sanity—a sanity that becomes a refuge for the worst kind of hatred of life—describes the essential process in a self without autonomy.

Regardless of whether one has been a rebel or opted for adjustment, what is involved here is the self-hatred of every person who has surrendered his or her self. Such capitulation brings with it the denial of one's own reality. It is in the hands of such people that morality becomes perverted.

Developing in this way, a person begins to fear his own impulses, and thus the need for approval and acceptance becomes of central concern. The struggle to be accepted for doing and being what is expected becomes a mechanism for evading inner anxiety. By locating life's meaning in approval, one renounces the possibility of being loved for the sake of one's true self. The very desire to be loved in this way becomes a source of self-contempt because wishing to be loved for one's own sensitivity would designate one as weak. Under such circumstances, as I have shown at length, children learn that love can be won only through docile maneuvering. But coming to terms with this situation leads to a secret contempt for the parents. In order to go on living with oneself and one's need for love, one must hate oneself, as well as everything reminiscent of authentic love. This is probably the underlying cause of cruelty. Neal Ascherson (1983) reports that Klaus Barbie, the Gestapo chief of Lyon, who tortured Jean Moulin to death, once said in an interview, "As I interrogated Jean Moulin, I felt he was myself." In other words, the more he saw himself, that is, that part of himself he had rejected, in Moulin, the more he had to hate and kill himself/Moulin.

By this process human beings sever themselves from their humanity. Thereafter they can be so torn apart by self-hatred that a complete conversion can take place in which a former compliant self may all of a sudden be hated by a new self that is just as nonautonomous as the earlier one.[2] This makes clear that an identity not rooted firmly in the development of an autonomous self is based solely on a system of abstractions that conceal an inner chaos.[3]

It may be, as I have outlined in the first chapter, that such people are the creators and advocates of the myth that suffering and sympathy are signs of weakness. They are the very ones held up to us as *strong* because they don't suffer! People with that kind of "strength," however, turn out to be cut off from their feelings because they *don't* have the strength to tolerate psychic pain. This perversion of the truth is often difficult to detect because the "strong," by seeing to it that they are in power, determine society's definition of "reality."

When such a view of reality becomes institutionalized, a man who accepts that view will kill another because he hates what he identifies as weakness in himself even though the so-called weakness is actually what is good about him. Milovan Djilas's autobiographical *Land Without Justice* (1958) tells about a Montenegrin who murders a Turk with whom he had just had a truly pleasant and satisfying encounter. Here we have a man who vents his rage because of abstract concepts of honor and manliness, concepts which have enslaved him. The murder occurred at a moment when the Turk was feeling secure because there was common ground between them; for the Montenegrin, however, although he had the same feeling, "something erupted inside . . . which he was utterly incapable of holding back."

Thus, it comes about that those in power, precisely because they are inwardly empty, manipulate whole nations, drawing people more and more into a morass of abstractions that smothers the oppressors, as well as the oppressed. "And a society which has come to wince at the very attempts to expose these methods by which it seeks to impose its will upon its members has already lost the feel of freedom and is on the path toward abolutism."[4] Such a society will attempt to camouflage its violence. As Solzhenitsyn put it in the unforgettable words of his 1970 Nobel lecture (1972): ". . . Let us not forget that violence does not have its own separate existence and is in fact incapable of having it: it is invariably interwoven with falsehood. . . . Violence finds its only refuge in falsehood, falsehood its only support in violence. Any man who has once acclaimed violence as his method must inexorably choose falsehood as his principle."

Nonautonomy has terrifying consequences for all of us. It is that state in which pursuit of power becomes the way of fending off inner chaos and the threat of psychotic disintegration. By spurning our inner world, turning our back on our ever-present feelings of impotence, and especially by our very striving for power itself, we merely deepen both our self-rejection and our fear of inner emptiness. As a result, we are left with no other choice but to step up our pursuit of power. Public power can thus become the goal, as well as a guarantor, of personal cohesion. The dynamics of this development permit no genuine compromises with other people. These pursuers of power regard any form of agreement as a sign of weakness in the other person; they don't believe in equality—one either dominates or is dominated. What they experienced in childhood has become the central lesson of their life: pain is the ruler of the mind, therefore only power counts. They can not admit of any other option, for if they did, they would have to concede the cowardice of their own original submission to pain.[5] *Yet it is their way of life that is invariably presented to us as realistic.* An existence like this is dedicated exclusively to death, since aliveness spells danger. And thus they reinforce the view that freedom brings with it an unrestrained self-assertion and is therefore dangerous. This has the effect of making those who rebel equate freedom with just such an uncurbed aggrandizement of the ego, which in turn confirms the worst fears of those who seek their identity in the possession and exercise of power!

It is this type of "realism" that is the true enemy of humanity. For purposes of self-preservation we must recognize it for what it is: a new (or extremely old?) form of madness, a flight into mental health, as Henry Miller describes it in Rimbaud's case. The power politics that is held up to us as realism is bringing the world closer to the abyss every day. It has always been so, only now those in power have unprecedented means of destruction at their disposal. And just as earlier, now too they try, by invoking the concept of realism, to disclaim the lethal consequences of their course of action and *the lethal state of mind leading to them.* The powers that be claim they want to protect us without any thought of self-interest, but as Nietzsche pointed out about philosophers in *Beyond Good and Evil,* there is no such thing as impersonality in human affairs. When statesmen (or stateswomen) are split in their being, they must continuously live with a lie. What they have to offer us then can only be something cut off from the sphere of humaneness. We will be able to recognize this fact, however, only if we ourselves stop seeking after gods, which means we have to free ourselves from the fears that caused us to locate godliness outside the boundaries of our own self. If we don't succeed, then rebellion will merely make us topple one church in order to erect another in its place, and power and its manifestations will endure, as Henry Miller pointed out. Under such conditions, we will only create new forms of tyranny.

It is sympathy and love that make possible the unfolding of the true self. Henry Miller expressed it poetically in his book on Rimbaud: " 'Everything we are taught is false,' Rimbaud protested in his youth. He was right, utterly right. But it is our mission on earth to combat false teaching by manifesting the truth which is in us. . . . The great miracle is to unite all men in the way of understanding. The key *is* Charity" (Miller 1956, p. 143).

There is no method or technique that leads to a real self. To expect such a thing is already the sign of a self that is an unconscious prisoner of the assumption that a human being is activated like a machine by pushing buttons. *Attitude* is the key to autonomy; we will find it if we allow our sympathy and love for others to flower. The paths leading to it are diverse because of the uniqueness of the individual; therefore, each of us will have to find his or her own path alone. Friends and supporters are essential, but the responsibility for the choice of a path must be our own. One must dare to experience one's own aliveness in order to learn that the phantoms blocking our path are actually powerless.

It is our fate, if we never had the chance to rebel, to live the absurdity of never having experienced a self of our own. "Who dies not before he dies is ruined when he dies," said Jakob Böhme, a sixteenth-century mystic and theosophist. But rebellion alone will not make a human being. It is only a first step on a long, difficult, and never-ending road toward overcoming our fear of the freedom to possess a self of our own along with a human heart.

NOTES

1. In this book Liedloff describes the way of life of the Yequana Indians of Venezuela. Here we see a form of child rearing that nurtures the human being's full potential for love and aliveness—rather than for power and death. In the passage quoted, Liedloff is showing how our culture fails in this respect.

2. The process by which kindness and tolerance are transformed into means of oppression and control is discussed further in my second chapter. Here I want to refer only to Christopher Lasch's *The Culture of Narcissism* (1979), in which he emphasizes the way tolerance on a social level can conceal a strict system of control. If children refuse to eat, for instance, the authority of the doctor is brought into play; if they are not obedient, a psychiatrist or psychologist is called in to help them with their "problem." In this manner, authority can be presented as the child's "friend" and "parents make their own problem—insubordination—the child's" (Lasch 1979, p. 182). What I am interested in, however, is the widespread violence engendered in people by crippling their autonomy—whether by direct or indirect, conscious or unconscious means. It is a violence unaware of its motives, and we see it on the rise everywhere—including in our children and in our schools. If only we are willing, we will be able to discern its origins. An English schoolteacher reports the following exchange in her classroom:

> "Who can tell me about the IRA? What is the conflict about in Northern Ireland?"
>
> "Oh, the Catholics hate the Protestants—can't we do something interestin'?"
>
> "If you're not interested, why do you support the IRA?"
>
> "Cor—because they throw bombs and smash things—blow people up—gr . . . reat!" (Hirsch, *New Statesman*)

The teacher comments: "It's the violence they like—not the human rights. It's their parents and teachers they hate—not the Protestants." This poem was written by one of her pupils:

> School is boring, school is mad.
> Soon I'm leaving, for that I'm glad.
> No more football, no more fun
> But I don't regret the things I've done.
> Smashing windows, breaking chairs
> Caned by teachers, but who cares?

The poem shows us that the deepest injury for children of our time—especially for the rebels among them—lies in their having joined their oppressors as a result of having lost their ability to perceive both their own and others' pain and suffering. They are however different from earlier generations: instead of espousing hypocritical values, these children espouse no values at all. I am grateful to Claus D. Eck for calling my attention to Pink Floyd's song "The Wall," which pinpoints the hypocrisy underlying this malaise:

> Hush now baby, don't you cry,
> Mama's gonna make all of your
> Nightmares come true,
> Mama's gonna keep you right here
> Under her wing,
> She won't let you fly but she might let you sing.

3. The concept of the "critical period" (as described by Scott in 1958, for example) is an extension of this way of thinking, with the basic idea, however, still remaining a mechanical one. According to Scott, there are critical times in development during which, provided the stimulus situation is favorable, patterns of behavior appropriate for that stage will be triggered. If not, this behavior formation will not appear. No consideration is given here to the possibility that the organism itself might have something to do with the failure to learn this new behavior. Yet Davis (1957) demonstrated in a now practically forgotten experiment that the reaction seeks out the stimulus! His work confirms and amplifies Piaget's idea that a stimulus doesn't become significant until it fits the scheme of an inner process (Flavel 1963).

4. McDougall (1928) was one of the first psychologists to deal with empathy. The research of Hygge (1976), who measured dermal resistance during empathic experiences, also deals with reciprocal human encounters (unfortunately only in a negative sense). It is interesting that Kenneth Clark, in a speech upon accepting an award from the American Psychological Association in 1980, argued for a renewed recognition of empathy as an important factor in human development. Empathy is significant for our purposes as the direct perception of another person's emotional state by means of the kinesthetic senses. Whatever cuts people off from their own emotionally tuned kinesthetic processes consequently cuts them off from direct perception of the emotional state of others. If an infant directly perceives something kinesthetically, such as the mother's fearfulness or her impatience, and she denies having such emotions or acts in a threatening way toward her child for expressing these perceptions, then the child's sense of helplessness will be so exacerbated that its empathy will become a burden. The complexity of this situation can be gathered from one of its variations. In an early psychoanalytical study, Stärke (1921) describes the contradictory and irreconcilable feelings of an infant who is sucking the mother's nipples, which are inflamed by nursing. Here, Stärke points out, the infant experiences at one and the same time *its* satisfaction and *her* pain.

5. Children's failure to thrive in life has already been described by Ribble (1943) and Shaheen et al. (1968). Schneirla (1959) provides the neurological basis for this. A constant flow of low-intensity stimuli via the afferent nerves is necessary, for example, to form and maintain the individual's metabolic pattern. In general, the differences in intensity of the stimulus flow to which infants are exposed are fundamental to the development of the essential characteristics of their subsequent arousal threshold.

6. The impossibility of influencing the environment in one's own favor heightens the helplessness already produced by learning that there is nothing to learn. The resulting helplessness probably causes a diminished vitality in the organism. Visintainer et al. (1982) report that rats in a control group showed a significantly reduced resistance to tumors when they were prevented from learning to evade stresses they were exposed to (it was made impossible for them to escape electrical shocks). Also of interest is an earlier experiment by Sklar and Anisman (1979), which demonstrates that *more prolonged* exposure to such shocks

restrengthened resistance to tumors. Perhaps an example of "adaptation" to helplessness?

7. Maier and Schneirla (1942) emphasize that contiguity learning (Pavlov's S-R) is of primary importance for the early stages of development. Yet selective learning must be postulated to account for the changing relationships of action to stimuli when endogenous conditions affect further adjustments.

8. So long as we cling to a concept of schizophrenia whose chief value lies merely in its usefulness in differential and diagnostic classification, we will be unable to appreciate the broader significance of this illness in the human scheme. It is my aim to place it in this wider context. Gaetano Benedetti (1972, 1976, 1983a, 1983b) has made fundamental contributions to opening the gates of our understanding in this area. His studies are marked not only by brilliance of formulation and depth of understanding for the schizophrenic but also by an extraordinary love for this suffering human being. It is this deep compassion—"a compassion without pity"—which expands our consciousness. His scientific studies furnish evidence that it is not clear thinking alone but love as well that brings about genuine knowledge of the human situation. For this reason he goes beyond (in the sense of "transcends") the boundaries of most large-scale studies in the field, which treat only bits and pieces of the schizophrenic experience and thus destroy the integrality of the information schizophrenic patients confront us with. Gustav Bychowski (1966), who was a student of Eugen Bleuler during World War I, often spoke of Bleuler and his emphasis on the moral aspects of schizophrenia, its drive for truth. These approaches give the concept of "schizophrenia" a much more inclusive meaning. The schizophrenic state is the end result of *struggling with*, and not *adapting oneself to*, the inhuman aspects of our life; this is why studying schizophrenia and the schizoid state can give us insight into the anatomy of the self. This view is also shared by Henry (1963, 1965), Laing (1959), and Siirala (1961), among others.

Another example of the same broadening of the concept of schizophrenia is found in the brilliant interpretation of Rainer Maria Rilke's *The Tale of the Love and Death of Cornet Christopher Rilke* by the psychoanalyst W. V. Silverberg (1947), who shows how the protagonist's helplessness, which led to a denial of the threatening world, is transformed into an affirmation of the all-inclusiveness of one's own psyche (such as we find in schizophrenics). In Rilke's prose poem the beleaguered hero experiences his heathen attackers' gleaming sabers as a laughing fountain whose spray falls gently upon him. This "schizoid maneuver" (Silverberg) is to a greater or lesser extent an aspect of every human relationship, for our fear of the individuality of the other person stems from our earlier childhood experiences when we were at the mercy of "loving" adults whose attempt to impose their will on us threatened to extinguish our own budding self.

9. F. Matthias Alexander suffered from speech disorders that almost caused him to lose his voice. For many pain-filled years he worked on his musculature, trying to improve his posture and movements. As a result of his efforts he also regained control of his voice. His method teaches us how to unlearn wrong habits.

10. In his study of the oppressed, Paulo Freire (1970, 1972) points out that they have internalized the image of the oppressor. Their goal as revolutionaries is the reversal of roles, not an authentic existence.

11. Henry Miller's text makes it clear that by "mother" he also means society as a whole.

12. It is interesting that Lenin recognized such demands as a form of infantile dependency. He wrote: "[They have] mistaken *their desire* . . . for actual fact. . . . [They] present impatience as a theoretically convincing argument" (Lenin 1972, pp. 41, 49).

13. Anna Freud's concept of identification with aggression (1946) is relevant here. She points out the defensive function of such an identification. I emphasize the way such a mechanism is directed against one's own potential center.

Chapter III

1. In his study of the psychology of power, the British political scientist Ronald V. Sampson (1966) describes this phenomenon with moral force and depth. He uses biographical evidence to demonstrate that the ambition of many successful men has been a reflection of their mothers' striving for power.

2. In Liedloff's study of the Yequana we also find an ability on the author's part to experience the reality of other people, something of which scientists are not always capable. Their ideology of self obstructs their vision. Since Liedloff did not see the Yequana with the "spe-

cialized" eyes of the anthropologist, she was free to perceive these people in a direct way.

3. Antill and Cunningham (1979) have described the way women base their self-esteem on "masculine" drives. The authors, themselves caught up in this myth, assume that the results of their research have to do with fundamental self-esteem rather than with that of a specific ambitious class of women. They are oblivious to the fact that what may be involved here is betrayal of one's own being or the disguising of hostility by identification with the male.

4. In his so-called "Checkers Speech," Nixon was so moved by his own words that he cried (Halberstam 1979). This is exactly what I have described: the real pain of others irritates people, whereas a deceptive maneuver, such as tearful eyes, fills them with the "power" of "generosity." They feel elated at the very moment that they are denying the truth and their own life. That is why Nixon's TV speech became a decisive factor in the success of his campaign for the vice presidency in 1952.

5. The quotations are taken from Elaine Pagels' *The Gnostic Gospels* (1979), an unusually perceptive work of Biblical scholarship concerning the discovery of two-thousand-year-old Gnostic manuscripts in 1945 near the town of Nag Hammadi in Upper Egypt.

6. Liedloff writes about this unstilled longing in her study of how human development becomes stunted: "These conditions, though they continue throughout [the child's] life, may go unnoticed for the simple reason that [it] cannot conceive of an alternative kind of relation of Self to Other" (Liedloff 1977, p. 71). This, however, is not correct in relation to learning about the uses of power.

Chapter IV

1. The following studies are seminal in this area: Blechschmidt (1977); Hebb (1958); Kuo (1932a, b, c, d, e and 1963); Lehrman (1953, 1965); Schneirla (1949, 1956, 1959, 1965).

2. Ribble, *The Rights of Infants*, Spitz and Wolf, "Smiling Response."

3. See Grunebaum, Freedman, and Greenblatt, "Sensory Deprivation"; Heron, Bexton, and Hebb, "Cognitive Effects"; Lilli, "Mental Effects."

Chapter V

1. The word "culture" is used here in its anthropological and sociological senses.

2. An allusion to Nietzsche's "arrows of longing for the other shore" (*Thus Spake Zarathustra*), quoted by Henry Miller in *The Time of the Assassins* (1956).

Chapter VI

1. Aronson and Rosenbloom (1971) observed that infants only thirty days old expressed pain and distress when confronted with an auditory-visual discrepancy in their perception of their mother. When her voice was displaced by means of a stereo amplifier system, the infant's unity of perception was impaired. Its resultant agitation and irritation furnish proof of its original integrative attitude and consequent need for synthesis.

2. Albert Speer's autobiography (1970) shows us the type of person who knows what ought to be felt, but who in fact feels nothing. Matthias Schmidt (1984) has unmasked Speer's true personality. How successful Speer was in manipulating his image can be seen from his obituary in the *New York Times* (2 September 1981), in which he was praised for his *humanity*. But Friedrich Percyval Reck-Malleczewen, a German conservative who was murdered by the Gestapo in 1945, described Speer as a man "who, in the projection of a 'positive' image, summed up the repellently mechanical boyishness of his generation" (1971). He recognized in Speer the soulless quality of a well-adjusted person without a self of his own. Joachim Fest (1970) describes Martin Bormann in similar terms: ". . . There is not a single event in Bormann's life that bears an individual stamp. . . ."

3. Michael Maccoby (1976) makes such connections clear in his description of today's leaders of industry but neglects to draw the consequences, since he himself identifies to a high degree with power and success. James Fallows (1981), former speechwriter for President Carter, describes such men in contemporary American politics in his study of the American army. (See also the remarks of Admiral Rickover

[1982].) John Newhouse's article on the aircraft industry in the *New Yorker* (1982) similarly describes men whose "reality" mirrors an unreal self. Since such people have adapted to the myth of success, however, no one sees through them, which has unfortunate consequences for all of us. In the field of science I would call attention to a case of fraud and plagiarism in medical literature that recently came to light (*Science,* 1980, 1982): when a physician and scientist, whose article was read and rejected by the editor of a medical journal only to appear later under the editor's own name, lodged a complaint, she was initially decried as petty by other professors and editors. Of course, anyone who had published two hundred articles in a decade and defended the guilty editor must be right! The worst of it was that the academic institutions involved in the case attempted to justify this type of fraud by ascribing it to the pressure to be successful! We can easily understand this if we see to what extent *image* has taken the place of true feelings. A new president of the American Association for the Advancement of Science was introduced to his colleagues in the Association's weekly periodical *Science* as having the following credentials: he is not only a professor and chairman of a university department but in addition chairman of a national committee comprising two hundred other scientists, chairman of several international committees, adviser to various government agencies, technical adviser to several laboratories, editor of *six* international scientific periodicals, and member of the board of directors of a number of important industrial firms. Then, at the end of this exhausting list we are assured that this man still has room in his life for his family and for amusement. Given such attachment to the image, is it any wonder that we fail to recognize people without a self and without true feelings?

Afterword

1. We must understand that Henry Miller means mother and/or father here, that the father becomes a symbol of the bad mother and later of a society characterized by rejection and denial.
2. The historian Erich Kahler (1956) points out that the Apostle Paul's conversion, which suddenly transformed his hatred of Christianity into hatred of Jewish law, was just such a turning against the former self.
3. This is actually the case with psychopaths. Apparent sanity masks a destructive inner rage, discernible only when it breaks out suddenly

and unexpectedly. But a person in power will scarcely ever be labelled psychopathic. The American psychiatrist Hervey Cleckley describes this phenomenon, which is usually concealed from the observer, in a study with the telling title *The Mask of Sanity* (1964).

4. Learned Hand, judge of the U.S. Court of Appeals, in his acquittal of Judith Coplon, whom the government charged with treason on account of her ideas (United States v. Coplon, 185 F.2d 629 [2d Cir. 1950]).

5. When the official self no longer functions and the promises guaranteeing identity disintegrate under the pressure of extreme disruptions (e.g., in the Middle Ages the Black Death, as described by Norman Cohn [1972]; and in today's age the universal threat of general economic collapse or nuclear annihilation), then people revolt *against* the forms that have been violently imposed upon them. We can learn the truth about the whole situation only from those lowest on the ladder of a given power's hierarchy, since they are the least conscious of the paradox of their position. In interviews with members of Somoza's National Guard in a Nicaraguan prison, Marie Luise Kaltenegger (1982) records the remarks of those whose self has no center. An instructor from the former death squad EEBI describes the training: "To teach somebody to obey orders, they make him do humiliating things. To stand there, for example, and on command to bleat like a sheep. . . . To have the whole platoon kick him in the butt . . . until he learns he's to ask no questions. . . ." A man who had been through the training reported: "I'm small and thin. Before I joined the National Guard, I was afraid of everything and everybody . . . [but now] I'm not afraid, that's the most important thing. . . . That's what I call being a man." Another: "I didn't have any shoes. . . . In the army they give you a uniform, boots, food, a bed. I liked it in the army. The National Guard was o.k." In answer to the observation that the people said the National Guard was a corrupt pack of murderers came the response: "The people are full of shit. The people lie. Yesterday they were for Somoza, today they're for the Sandinistas. What the people say doesn't count." Concerning the fact that the captured Somoza supporters were not executed: ". . . I don't understand it. Why [do they burden themselves] with thousands of deadly enemies? I don't think the Sandinistas have learned anything. . . . They're just civilians." In other words, if an opponent is humane, he's a weak idiot! That goes against the speaker's grain because it confronts him with his own rejected humanity.

BIBLIOGRAPHY

Alexander, F. Matthias. *Man's Supreme Inheritance*. London: Chaterton, 1910.

_____. *The Use of the Self*. Manchester: Re-Education Pub., 1932.

Antill, J. K., and Cunningham, J. D. "Self-Esteem as a Function of Masculinity in Both Sexes." *Journal of Consulting and Clinical Psychology* 4 (1979).

Arendt, Hannah. *Eichmann in Jerusalem: A Report on the Banality of Evil*. New York: Viking Press, 1963.

Aronson, E., and Rosenbloom, S. "Space Perception in Early Infancy: Perception within a Common Auditory-Visual Space." *Science* 172 (1971).

Ascherson, Neal. "The 'Bildung' of Barbie." *New York Review of Books*, 24 November 1983.

Ashton-Warner, Sylvia. *Teacher*. New York: Simon & Schuster, 1963.

Ball, Hugo. *Zur Kritik der deutschen Intelligenz*. Munich: Rogner & Bernhard, 1970.

Baumann, Bommie. *Terror or Love?* New York: Grove Press, 1977.

Benedetti, Gaetano. "The Irrational in the Psychotherapy of Psychosis." *Journal of the American Academy of Psychoanalysis* 1 (1979).

_____. *Der Geisteskranke als Mitmensch*. Göttingen: Vandenhoeck & Ruprecht, 1976.

_____. "Possibilities and Limits of Individual Psychotherapy of Schizophrenic Patients." In *Psychosocial Intervention in Schizophrenia*, edited by H. Stierlin; L. C. Wynne; and M. Wirsching. Berlin: Springer, 1983a.

────────. *Todeslandschaften der Seele.* Göttingen: Vandenhoeck & Ruprecht, 1983b.

Bernfeld, S. "On Psychoanalytic Training." *Psychoanalytic Quarterly* 31 (1962).

Bettelheim, Bruno. "Individual and Mass Behavior in Extreme Situations." In *Readings in Social Psychology,* edited by E. Maccoby. New York: Holt, Rinehart & Winston, 1958.

────────. *The Informed Heart: The Human Condition in Modern Mass Society.* London: Thames & Hudson, 1961.

Birch, H. G. Unpublished, quoted by Schneirla (1956).

────────. Lecture. Department of Post-Graduate Psychology, New York University, 21 March 1950.

Blackney, Raymond B. *Meister Eckhart: A Modern Translation.* New York: Harper & Row, 1941.

Blechschmit, Erich. *The Beginnings of Human Life.* Translated by Transemantics, Inc. New York: Springer-Verlag, 1977.

Bone, Evelyne. *Seven Years Solitary.* New York: Harcourt Brace, 1957.

Bruner, Jerome; Oliver, R.; Greenfield, P.; et al. *Studies in Cognitive Growth.* New York: John Wiley & Sons, 1966.

Butler, Samuel. *The Way of All Flesh.* New York: Modern Library, 1950.

Bychowski, Gustav. Personal statement to author, 1966.

Byrd, Richard E. *Alone.* New York: Putnam, 1938.

Chekhov, Anton. *Letters of Anton Chekhov.* Selected and edited by Avrahm Yarmolinsky. Translated by Bernard Guilbert Guerny, Lynn Solotaroff, and Avrahm Yarmolinsky. New York: Viking Press, 1973.

Clark, Kenneth B. "Empathy, a Neglected Topic in Psychological Research." *American Psychologist* 35 (1980).

Cleckley, Hervey. *The Mask of Sanity.* St. Louis: C. V. Mosby, 1964.

Cohn, Norman. *The Pursuit of the Millennium.* New York: Oxford University Press, 1972.

Condon, W. S., and Sander, L. W. "Neonate Movement Is Synchronized with Adult Speech: Interactional Participation and Language Acquisition." *Science* 183 (1974).

"Coping with Fraud." *Science* (1982b).

Davis, R. C. "Differences in Response Patterns: Results and Problems." *Transactions of the New York Academy of Sciences* 19 (1957).

DeCasper, A. J., and Fifer, W. P. "Of Human Bonding: Newborns Prefer Their Mothers' Voices." *Science* 208 (1980).

Denenberg, V. "Critical Periods, Stimulus Input, and Emotional Reactivity: A Theory of Infantile Stimulation." *Psychological Review* 71 (1964).

Des Pres, Terrence. *The Survivor: An Anatomy of Life in the Death Camps.* New York: Oxford University Press, 1976.

Deutsch, H. " Über einen Typus der Pseudoaffektivität ('Als ob')." *Internationale Zeitschrift für Psychoanalyse* 20 (1934).

_____. "Some Forms of Emotional Disturbance and Their Relationship to Schizophrenia." *Psychoanalytic Quarterly* 11 (1942).

Dinesen, Isak. *Out of Africa.* New York: Modern Library, 1952.

Djilas, Milovan. *Land Without Justice.* New York: Harcourt Brace, 1958.

"Emergence of a Fraud." *Science* (1980a).

Erdheim, M. "Nach aller Regel." *Kursbuch* 63 (1981).

Erikson, Erik H. *Young Man Luther: A Study in Psychoanalysis and History.* New York: W. W. Norton, Norton Library, 1962.

_____. "Inner and Outer Space: Reflections on Womanhood." In *The Woman in America,* edited by Robert J. Lifton. Boston: Houghton Mifflin, 1964.

Fallows, James. "The Great Defense Deception." *New York Review of Books,* 29 May 1981.

Farber, Leslie. *The Ways of the Will.* New York: Basic Books, 1966.

Feldenkrais, Moshe. *Body and Mature Behavior.* New York: International Universities Press, 1973.

_____. *Awareness through Movement.* New York: Harper & Row, 1972.

_____. *The Case of Nora.* New York: Harper & Row, 1977.

Fest, Joachim C. *The Face of the Third Reich: Portraits of Nazi Leadership.* Translated by Michael Bullock. New York: Pantheon, 1970.

Fester, Richard; König, Marie E. P.; Jonas, Doris F.; and Jonas, A. David. *Weib und Macht: Fünf Millionen Jahre Urgeschichte der Frau.* Frankfurt: Fischer, 1979.

Flavell, John H. *The Developmental Psychology of Jean Piaget.* New York: Van Nostrand, 1963.

Frankl, Viktor. *Man's Search for Meaning: An Introduction to Logotherapy.* Translated by Ilse Lasch. Boston: Beacon Press, 1968.

Freire, Paulo. "Cultural Action for Freedom." *Harvard Educational Review* 40, 3 (1970).

——. *Pedagogy of the Oppressed.* New York: Herder & Herder, 1972.

Freud, Anna. *The Ego and the Mechanisms of Defense.* New York: International Universities Press, 1946.

Frisch, Max. *Sketchbook, 1966–1971.* Translated by Geoffrey Skelton. New York: Harcourt Brace Jovanovich, 1974.

Fromm, Erich. *Escape from Freedom.* New York: Holt, Rinehart, & Winston, 1941.

Fuller, J. L. "Experiential Deprivation and Later Behavior." *Science* 158 (1967).

Gilman, Charlotte Perkins. *The Yellow Wallpaper.* Old Westbury, N.Y.: Feminist Press, 1973.

Gorer, Geoffrey. "Man Has No 'Killer' Instinct." *New York Times Magazine,* 26 November 1966.

Gruen, Arno. "Autonomy and Identification: The Paradox of Their Opposition." *International Journal of Psycho-Analysis* 49 (1968).

——. "The Oedipal Experience and the Development of the Self." *Psychoanalytic Review* 56 (1969).

——. "The Discontinuity in the Ontogeny of Self: Possibilities for Integration or Destructiveness." *Psychoanalytic Review* 61 (1974).

——. "Autonomy and Compliance: The Fundamental Antithesis." *Journal of Humanistic Psychology* 16 (1976).

——. "On Abstraction: The Reduction and Destruction of Human Experience." *Journal of Humanistic Psychology* 18 (1978).

——. "Lernen und Lebenslust: Unvereinbar?" Originally published as "Lernen ohne Anstrengung." *Neue Zürcher Zeitung,* 5–6 July 1980a.

——. "Maternal Rejection and Children's Intensity." *Confinia Psychiatrica* 23 (1980b).

Gruen, Arno, and Hertzman, Max. "Autonomy and Compliance." *Dynamische Psychiatrie* 16 (1972).

Grunebaum, H. U.; Freedman, S. J.; and Greenblatt, M. "Sensory Deprivation and Personality." *American Journal of Psychiatry* 116 (1960).

Halberstam, David. *The Powers That Be.* New York: Knopf, 1979.

Hanley, William. *Slow Dance on the Killing Ground.* New York: Random House, 1964.

Harris, David. *Goliath.* New York: Avon, 1970.

"Harvard Delays in Reporting Fraud." *Science* (1982a).

Hebb, D. O. "The Motivating Effects of Exteroceptive Stimulation." *American Psychologist* 13 (1958).

Henry, Jules. *Culture against Man.* New York, Random House, 1963.

_____. *Pathways to Madness.* New York: Random House, 1965.

Heron, W.; Bexton, W. H.; and Hebb, D. O. "Cognitive Effects of a Decreased Variation in the Sensory Environment. *American Psychologist* 18 (1953).

Hirsch, Muriel. "To Sir, with Hate." *New Statesman* (London), 20 October 1972.

Höss, Rudolf. *Commandant of Auschwitz: The Autobiography of Rudolf Höss.* Translated by Constantine FitzGibbon. Cleveland and New York: World Publishing, 1959.

Hygge, S. "Emotional and Electrodermal Reactions to the Suffering of Another." *Acta Universitatis Upsaliensis* 2 (1976).

Jacoby, Russell. *Social Amnesia: A Critique of Conformist Psychology from Adler to Laing.* Boston: Beacon Press, 1975.

Kahler, Erich. *Man the Measure.* New York: George Braziller, 1956.

Kaltenegger, Marie Luise. "Als Soldat und brav." *Kursbuch* 67 (1982).

Kavanau, J. L. "Behavior of Captive White Feeted Mice." *Science* 155 (1967).

Kempinski, Antonio. *Rytm Zycia.* Cracow: Wydawnictwo Literatckie, 1973.

Kierkegaard, Søren. *The Sickness unto Death.* Translated by Walter Lowrie. New York: Doubleday, 1954.

_____. *The Present Age.* Translated by Alexander Dru. New York: Harper & Row, 1962.

Kohut, Heinz. *The Restoration of the Self.* New York: International Universities Press, 1977.

Krutch, Joseph Wood. *The Measure of Man: On Freedom, Human Values, Survival, and Modern Temper.* 2d ed. New York: Bobbs-Merrill, Charter Books, 1962.

Kuo, Z. Y. "The Influence of Embryonic Movements upon the Behavior after Hatching." *Journal of Comparative Psychology* 14 (1932a).

_____. "The Mechanical Factors in the Various Stages Leading to Hatching." *Journal of Experimental Zoology* 62 (1932b).

_____. "Ontogeny of Embryonic Behavior in Aves: I. The Chronology and General Nature of the Behavior of the Chick Embryo." *Journal of Experimental Zoology* 61 (1932c).

_____. "The Reflex Concept in the Light of Embryonic Behavior in Birds." *Psychological Review* 39 (1932d).

_____. "The Structure and Environmental Factors in Embryonic Behavior." *Journal of Comparative Psychology* 13 (1932e).

_____. "Total Patterns, Local Reflexes, or Gradients of Response?" In *Proceedings of the Sixteenth International Congress of Zoology* (Washington, D.C.) 4 (1963).

Kükelhaus, Hugo. *Unmenschliche Architektur.* Cologne: Gaia, 1978.

Laing, R. D. *The Divided Self.* London: Tavistock, 1959.

_____. *The Politics of Experience.* New York: Ballantine, 1968.

Lasch, Christopher. *The Culture of Narcissism.* New York: W. W. Norton, 1979.

Latané, B., and Darley, J. "Bystander 'Apathy.'" *American Scientist* 57 (1969).

Lawrence, D. H. *The Rainbow.* Harmondsworth: Penguin, 1949.

_____. *Women in Love.* Harmondsworth: Penguin, 1960.

Lehrman, D. S. "A Critique of Konrad Lorenz's Theory of Instinctive Behavior." *Quarterly Review of Biology* 28 (1953).

_____. "Interaction between Internal and External Environments in the Regulation of the Reproductive Cycle of the Ring Dove." In *Sex and Behavior,* edited by F. A. Beach. New York: John Wiley & Sons, 1965.

Lenin, V. I. *"Left-Wing" Communism: An Infantile Disorder.* New York: International Publishers, 1972.

Liedloff, Jean. *The Continuum Concepts: Allowing Human Nature to Work Successfully.* rev. ed. Reading, Mass.: Addison-Wesley, 1977.

Lilli, J. C. "Mental Effects of Reduction of Ordinary Levels of Physical Stimuli on Intact, Healthy Persons." *Psychiatric Research Reports* 5 (1956).

Maccoby, Michael. *The Gamesman: The New Corporate Leaders.* New York: Simon & Schuster, 1976.

McDougall, William. *An Introduction to Social Psychology.* Boston: J. W. Luce, 1926.

Maier, N. R. F., and Schneirla, T. C. "Mechanisms in Conditioning. *Psychology Review* 49 (1942).

Manvell, Roger, and Fraenkel, Heinrich. *The Incomparable Crime: Mass Extermination in the Twentieth Century: The Legacy of Guilt.* London: Heinemann, 1967.

Marcuse, Herbert. *One-Dimensional Man: Studies in the Ideology of Advanced Industrial Society.* Boston: Beacon Press, 1964.

Milgram, S. "Behavioral Study of Obedience." *Journal of Abnormal and Social Psychology* 67 (1963).

Miller, Alice. *The Drama of the Gifted Child: How Narcissistic Parents Form and Deform the Emotional Lives of Their Talented Children.* Translated by Ruth Ward. New York: Basic Books, 1981.

_____. *For Your Own Good: Hidden Cruelty in Child-Rearing and the Roots of Violence.* Translated by Hildegarde Hannum and Hunter Hannum. New York: Farrar, Straus & Giroux, 1983.

Miller, Henry. *The Time of the Assassins.* New York: New Directions, 1956.

_____. *Black Spring.* New York: Grove Press, 1963.

Muhr, Caroline. *Freundinnen.* Munich: Franz Schneekluth, 1974.

Nash, Henry T. "The Bureaucratization of Homicide." *The Bulletin of the Atomic Scientists* 36 (1980).

Newhouse, John. "The Aircraft Industry—Part II." *New Yorker,* 21 June 1982.

O'Neill, Eugene. *More Stately Mansions.* New Haven: Yale University Press, 1964.

Bibliography

Ortega y Gasset, José. *The Dehumanization of Art and Other Writings on Art and Culture.* Garden City, N.Y.: Doubleday, Anchor Books, 1956.

Orwell, George. "In Front of Your Nose." In *The Collected Essays, Journalism and Letters of George Orwell,* edited by Sonia Orwell and Ian Angus, vol. 4. London: Secker & Warburg, 1968.

Pagels, Elaine. *The Gnostic Gospels.* New York: Random House, 1979.

Pawelczyńska, Anna. *Values and Violence in Auschwitz: A Sociological Analysis.* Translated by Catherine S. Leach. Berkeley: University of California Press, 1979.

Payne, Robert. *The Civil War in Spain.* New York: Premier Books, 1962.

Phillips, D. P. "Motor Vehicle Fatalities Increase Just after Publicized Suicide Stories." *Science* 196 (1977).

————. "Airplane Accident Fatalities Increase Just after Newspaper Stories about Murder and Suicide. *Science* 201 (1978).

"President Elect." *Science,* Feb. 22, 1980.

Reck-Malleczewen, Friedrich Percyval. *Tagebuch eines Verzweifelten.* Frankfurt: Fischer, 1971.

Ribble, Margaretha A. *The Rights of Infants: Early Psychological Needs and Their Satisfaction.* New York: Columbia University Press, 1943.

Rickover, Hyman G. "Advice from Admiral Rickover." *New York Review of Books,* 18 March 1982.

Rimbaud, Arthur. *Illuminations: A New American Translation.* Translated by Bertrand Mathieu. Brockport, N.Y.: BOA Editions, 1979.

Robinson, James McConkey. *The Nag Hammadi Library.* New York: Harper & Row, 1977.

Roffwarg, H. P.; Muzio, J. N.; and Dement, W. C. "Ontogenetic Development of the Human Sleep-Dream Cycle." *Science* 152 (1966).

Rosenblatt, J. S. "The Basis of Early Responses to the Mother, Siblings, and the Home and Nest in the Altrical Young of Selected Species of Subprimate Mammals." Report, Institute of Animal Behavior, Rutgers University, 1978.

Sampson, Ronald V. *The Psychology of Power.* New York: Pantheon, 1966.

Schmidt, Matthias. *Albert Speer: The End of a Myth.* Translated by Joachim Neugroschel. New York: St. Martin's Press, 1984.

Schneirla, T. C. "Levels in the Psychological Capacities of Animals." In *Philosophy for the Future*, edited by R. W. Sellars; V. J. McGill; and M. Farber. New York: Macmillan, 1949.

──────. "Interrelationships of the 'Innate' and the 'Acquired' in Instinctive Behavior." In *L'Instinct dans le comportement des animaux et de l'homme*, edited by P. Brassé. Paris: Masson, 1956.

──────. "An Evolutionary and Developmental Theory of Biphasic Processes Underlying Approach and Withdrawal." In *Nebraska Symposium on Motivation*, edited by M. R. Jones. Lincoln, Neb.: University of Nebraska Press, 1959.

──────. "Aspects of Stimulation and Organization in Approach/Withdrawal Processes Underlying Vertebrate Behavioral Development." In *Advances in the Study of Behavior*, edited by D. S. Lehrman; R. Hinde; and E. Shaw. New York: Academic Press, 1965.

Scholl, Ilse. *Die Weisse Rose*. Frankfurt: Fischer, 1977.

Schuls Klaus-Peter. *Kurt Tucholsky*. Reinbek: Rowohlt, 1959.

Scott, J. P. "Critical Periods in the Development of Social Behavior in Puppies." *Psychosomatic Medicine* 20 (1958).

Shaheen, E.; Alexander, D.; Truskowsky M.; and Barbero, J. "Failure to Thrive: A Retrospective Profile." *Clinical Pediatry* 7 (1968).

Siirala, Martti. *Die Schizophrenie des Einzelnen und der Allgemeinheit*. Göttingen: Vandenhoeck & Ruprecht, 1961.

Silverberg, W. V. "The Schizoid Maneuver." *Psychiatry* 10 (1947).

Skinner, B. F. *Beyond Freedom and Dignity*. New York: Knopf, 1971.

Sklar, L. S., and Anisman, H. "Stress and Coping Factors Influence Tumor Growth." *Science* 205 (1979).

Solzhenitsyn, Alexander. *1970 Nobel Lecture*. Stockholm: Nobel Foundation, 1972.

──────. *The Gulag Archipelago 1918–1956*. Translated by Thomas P. Whitney. New York: Harper & Row, 1973.

Speer, Albert. *Inside the Third Reich: Memoirs*. Translated by Richard Winston and Clara Winston. New York: Macmillan, 1970.

Spitz, R., and Wolf, K. M. "The Smiling Response: A Contribution to the Ontogenesis of Social Relations." *Genetic Psychology Monographs* 34 (1946).

Stärke, A. "The Castration Complex." *International Journal of Psychoanalysis* 2 (1921).

Stillman, Edmund O. "Civilian Sanctuary and Target Avoidance Policy in Thermonuclear War." *Annals of the American Academy of Political and Social Science* 392 (1970).

Sullivan, J. W. N. *Beethoven.* New York: Vintage, 1960.

Szent-Györgyi, A. "Teaching and the Expanding Knowledge." *Science* 146 (1964).

Tinbergen, N. "Ethology and Stress Disease." *Science* 185 (1974).

Traven, B. *The Death Ship: The Story of an American Sailor.* New York: L. Hill, 1973.

Tuchman, Barbara. *Stilwell and the American Experience in China.* New York: Macmillan, 1971.

Turnbull, Colin M. *The Forest People.* New York: Simon & Schuster, 1962.

Vaillant, G. E. "Natural History of Male Psychological Health: VI. Correlates of Successful Marriage and Fatherhood." *American Journal of Psychiatry* 135 (1978).

Visintainer, M. A.; Volpicelli, J. R.; and Seligman, M. E. P. "Tumor Rejection in Rats after Inescapable or Escapable Shock." *Science* 216 (1982).

von Holst, E., and Mittelstaedt, H. "Das Reafferenzprinzip: Wechselwirkung zwischen Zentralnervensystem und Peripherie." *Naturwissenschaft* 37 (1950).

Vuorenkoski, V.; Wasz-Höckert, O.; Koivisto, E.; and Lind, J. "The Effects of Cry Stimulus on the Temperature of the Lactating Breast of Primipara." *Experientia* 25 (1969).

Wald, George. "America's My Home: Not My Business, My Home." *Bulletin of the Atomic Scientists* 35 (1969).

Wasserman, Jakob. *The World's Illusion.* Translated by Ludwig Lewisohn. 2 vols. New York: Harcourt, Brace & Co., 1920.

White, Theodore H. *Breach of Faith: The Fall of Richard Nixon.* New York: Atheneum, 1975.

Whitehead, Alfred North. *Science and the Modern World.* New York: Macmillan, 1925.

Wieder, S. *The Texture of Early Maternal Experience: Maternal Control and Affect in Relation to the Second Year of Life*. City University of New York. New York: University Microfilms, 1972.

Wilson, Colin. *The Outsider.* New York: Houghton Mifflin, 1956.

Wilson, Edmund. *The Wound and the Bow.* New York: Oxford University Press, 1965.

Zweig, Stefan. *The Royal Game and Other Stories.* Translated by Jill Sutcliffe. New York: Harmony Books, 1981.

INDEX